# The Killing of Chester Bartell

Norman K. (Ken) Hunt

Publisher: Cowboy Miner Productions
1614 E. Bell Road, Ste. 101 #33
Phoenix, AZ 85022
Phone: (602) 569-6063
www.CowboyMiner.com

**Publisher's Cataloging-in-Publication Data**
Hunt, Norman K., 1934—
The Killing of Chester Bartell
Norman K. Hunt.
p. cm. Illustrated.

ISBN: 978-1-931725-21-7

1. Bartell, Chester. 2. Trials—Western. 3. Western History.
4. Ranching. 5. Murders—Western. 6. Animas Valley, NM—History
I. Title

Library of Congress Control Number: 2006922053

Book Design & Typesetting: SageBrush Publications, Tempe, Arizona
Jacket Design: ATG Productions, Phoenix, Arizona
Printing: Friesens Corporation
Printed in Canada

# Contents

Dedicated to the memory of my late brother, Joseph Phillip Hunt—
cowboy, master story teller, mentor, best friend
and the nicest man I ever knew.

# Introduction

On September 13, 1917, three Hunt brothers, Jack, Sam and Joe, began driving a small herd of cattle across their ranch at the western edge of New Mexico's Animas Valley. The Hunts had become involved in a dispute with some of their neighbors, and their adversaries had recently begun harassing them. On several recent occasions, one or more of their hostile neighbors had come on to the Hunt ranch and, from concealed positions, had directed rifle fire at or near the Hunts. As Jack, Sam and Joe rode along that morning, they were angry and wary—and armed with pistols and rifles.

As they neared the top of a ridge, Jack briefly left the trail to retrieve some cows that had strayed. Sam and Joe continued along the trail to where it forked around a dense clump of brush. Skulking behind the brush on his horse was one Chester Bartell. As Sam and Joe rode around either side of the clump of brush, they spotted Bartell reaching for his rifle. Sam and Joe drew their pistols, opened fire on Bartell and killed him instantly. And so began, for Sam and Joe, a gut-wrenching series of encounters with the criminal justice system—an ordeal that would continue for seven agonizing years.

SILVER CITY
90
ARIZONA
NEW MEXICO
LORDSBURG
10
338
AREA MAP
9
ANIMAS
RODEO
SULFER SPRINGS VALLEY
ANIMAS VALLEY
80
BISBEE
DOUGLAS
CLOVERDALE
USA
SAN BERNARDINO RANCH
MEXICO
SONORA
CHIHUAHUA
VICINITY MAP
5
10
20 miles

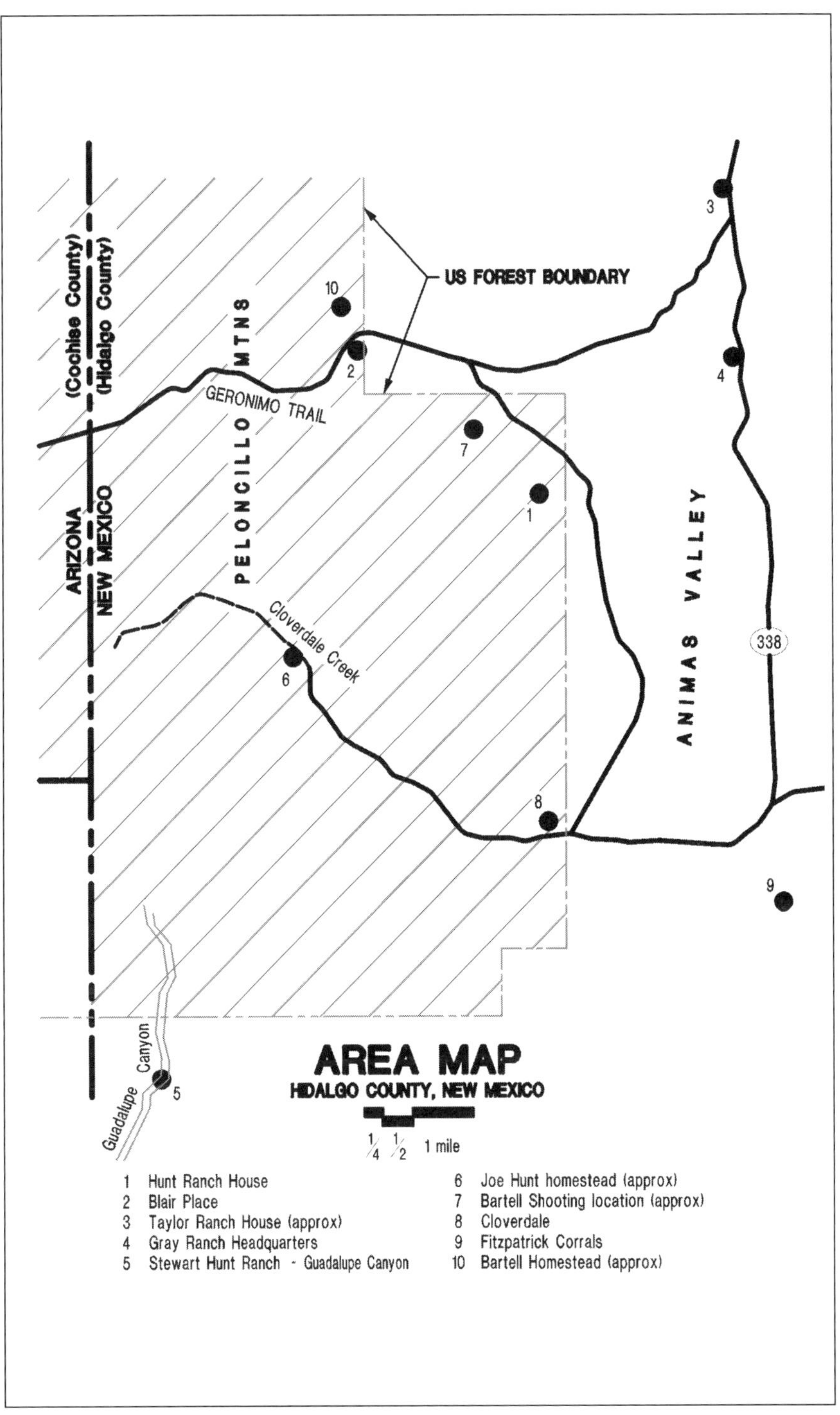
US FOREST BOUNDARY
(Cochise County)
(Hidalgo County)
ARIZONA
NEW MEXICO
PELONCILLO MTNS
GERONIMO TRAIL
Cloverdale Creek
ANIMAS VALLEY
338
Guadalupe Canyon
AREA MAP
HIDALGO COUNTY, NEW MEXICO
1/4 1/2 1 mile
1 Hunt Ranch House
2 Blair Place
3 Taylor Ranch House (approx)
4 Gray Ranch Headquarters
5 Stewart Hunt Ranch - Guadalupe Canyon
6 Joe Hunt homestead (approx)
7 Bartell Shooting location (approx)
8 Cloverdale
9 Fitzpatrick Corrals
10 Bartell Homestead (approx)

# How This Came About

I am the son of Joseph Stuart Hunt, one of the three brothers charged with murdering Chester Bartell. While growing up, I heard occasional references to the "troubles"—the killing of Chester Bartell and related events. This whole matter of the "troubles" was an unpleasant chapter in the family's experience. That, together with their inherent stoicism, made our elders reluctant to discuss it. Their reticence only heightened my curiosity. Others in my generation also heard something of the "troubles," but, as with me, it wasn't much.

In connection with another matter, I was in Albuquerque in 1972. There, I met a lawyer named Ryan, who happened to be the son of Raymond R. Ryan, the presiding judge at the first murder trial in Silver City. The younger Ryan had grown up in Silver City and, no doubt through his father, knew of the murder trials, which ensued from the Bartell killing. He had bound volumes of the New Mexico Supreme Court's Reports in his office library, and he made me copies of the two reports relating to the two appeals in New Mexico v. Hunt et al. This was my first encounter with the written record of the two cases. With the minor exception of some of the precedent citations, these two reports are transcribed herein in their entirety. One of these reports appears in the chapter titled, The Second Appeal, and the other is included as Appendix A.

I read over the two Supreme Court reports soon after receiving them in Albuquerque, and shared them with some other family members, but did little else in the way of research on the Bartell matter until 2004. By that time I had been retired for several years, and had been working with others, notably my cousin, Betty (Hunt) Kaye, on the Hunt family's history. In May 2004 I met Diana Hadley, Director of the Office of Ethnohistorical Research at the Arizona State Museum on the University of Arizona Campus in Tucson. Ms. Hadley had lived on the ranch once owned by Stewart Hunt in Guadalupe Canyon. Her former husband, Drummond Hadley, still lives there. Ms. Hadley expressed an interest in the Hunt family history and knew of the Bartell killing. She gave me copies of two old newspaper clippings about the killing. This tweaked my interest in the Bartell matter, and I decided to begin researching it in earnest. My initial intent was to put together a modest treatise on the Bartell matter for distribution within the family.

In June 2004, in the valued company of my good friend, Chloe Kavanaugh, I drove to Silver City, New Mexico, the site of the first (1918) murder trial. There, we visited the Grant County Court House, and found that the court files there no longer contained anything on the first murder trial. The court officials in Silver City were cooperative, but their old files had either been discarded or sent to the New Mexico State Record Center and Archives in Santa Fe. We next checked at the museum in Silver City, and here we had much better luck. The museum had microfilm copies of old issues of the Silver City newspapers, and we found and copied several articles about the 1918 murder trial. One article, that had been published in the *Silver City Independent* on April 9, 1918, was particularly good. A transcription of that article is included as Appendix B.

On the way back home to Phoenix, we stopped by the Hidalgo County Court House in Lordsburg, New Mexico. Here we found and copied court records for both the first (Silver City) and the second (Lordsburg, 1921) trials. These records were not complete, but they did contain some useful information. At this Court House we also found and copied some newspaper articles about the second trial that had appeared in the *Lordsburg Liberal.* Appendix C is a transcription of one of those articles, published on May 26, 1921.

In July 2004 I met again with Diana Hadley and picked up some more useful information, including how to contact her former spouse, Drummond (Drum) Hadley. After an exchange of letters, e-mails and telephone calls, I was able to make arrangements with Mr. Hadley to visit him at his Guadalupe Canyon Ranch. Accompanied by Bill Nowlin, I visited Guadalupe Canyon in November. Bill is a cousin, another Hunt descendent and a close friend. Drum was very hospitable. He has lived in Guadalupe Canyon for about thirty-five years, knows the area well, and was generous with that knowledge. The value of this visit was later found to be somewhat diminished by the fact that at the time we were operating on the mistaken belief that the shooting of Chester Bartell had occurred on the Guadalupe Canyon Ranch.

Over the next several months I completed the first draft of this book, and had made preliminary arrangements for its publication. However, I was uneasy with the draft, because the information on which it was based seemed shaky. My sources for this information were several articles in small town newspapers, some sketchy court records, useful but not very specific data from the Hadleys, and the even sketchier handed-down family lore taken from my own memory and from the memories of my brother and cousins.

By telephone, I had tried, without much success, to get a lead on any pertinent information on the Bartell matter, which may have been stored in the state archive center in Santa Fe. I finally decided that if I were to get any useful information from sources in Santa Fe, I would have to go there personally. Accordingly, Chloe Kavanaugh and I drove to Santa Fe in April 2005. We first stopped by the offices of the New Mexico State Record Center and Archives. The folks there were friendly but were unable to find anything in their records concerning the killing of Chester Bartell. They did recommend that we contact a particular individual at the offices of the New Mexico Supreme Court, also in Santa Fe. We followed their recommendation and at the Supreme Court offices we found what we had been looking for. To our amazement, the Supreme Court had the complete records for both trials and the subsequent appeals on microfilm. Included were verbatim transcripts of the testimony in both trials, together with the appeal briefs, pleadings, witness lists, court orders, and other miscellany—a total of over 1,700 pages. The Supreme Court staff gave us access to a microfilm reader/printer, and in two hectic days we copied all of the 1,700 plus pages. Some truly hard data was now in hand.

The next task was reading and indexing the large pile of Supreme Court documents. I then went back over the entire draft and made the necessary corrections and additions for conformance with the new and better data from the Supreme Court records. It was a chore, but I am now able to present the story of the killing of Chester Bartell with greater confidence in its authenticity.

As with any such project, a lot of people contributed to the effort that went into this book, and at least a few must be acknowledged. Chloe Kavanaugh has inspired (and goaded) me throughout. As noted above, she joined me on several trips to New Mexico and helped sort through the various public records that we found there. Chloe also typed parts of the manuscript and thoroughly reviewed it all, several times. Bill Nowlin and I together explored Southeastern Arizona and Southwestern New Mexico on two separate trips. He too read over the manuscript and made useful comments. Bill also contributed bits of family lore, which he had picked up in conversations with his father and grandmother (my father's older sister, Caroline).

Three first cousins and myself are all that remain of our generation of Hunts. These three are Dorothy (Hunt) Finley, Betty (Hunt) Kaye and Tom Hunt. Dorothy and Tom are Jack Hunt's children, and Betty is the daughter of Jim Hunt. All three generously shared their knowledge of the family's history and, in particular, what they knew of the Bartell killing. Also useful was the posthumous contribution of my brother, Joe, coming in the form of "Joe's Notes" (see Bibliography).

My neighbor, Sydney Davis, twice reviewed and commented on the manuscript. Her input has been particularly valuable, since she is an attorney and retired prosecutor from the office of the Arizona Attorney General. Thankfully, she kept this layman from making several blunders in my commentary on the legal intricacies of New Mexico v. Hunt et al.

The two maps were skillfully drafted by Anthony S. Coscia. Tony is an old friend. Finally, I must recognize the very good work of Janice Coggin, owner and manager of my publisher, Cowboy Miner Productions.

*Norman K. Hunt*
*Phoenix, Arizona*
*January 2006*

# Background

Charles P. (C.P.) Hunt and his wife Susan Mary had a total of ten children. They were:

| Name | Born |
|---|---|
| Lucy | 1871 |
| Caroline | 1873 |
| Charles Harris | 1876 |
| James Wilkins | 1877 |
| Valerie (Dolly) | 1879 |
| John Partridge | 1881 |
| Samuel Leroy | 1885 |
| Bessie Mary | 1888 |
| Nellie Susan | 1892 |
| Joseph Stuart | 1895 |

With the exception of the oldest daughter, Lucy, the entire family relocated from Central Texas to Southeastern Arizona. Photo No. 1 on page 14 was taken in Bisbee, Arizona in April 1920 on the occasion of the 50$^{th}$ wedding anniversary of C. P. and Mary Susan Hunt. Except for Lucy, the photo includes all of their children.

*Family dinner on occasion of the 50th wedding anniversary for Charles Phillip and Susan Mary Hunt, on or about April 4, 1920 in Bisbee. Arizona: Standing, left to right, their five sons: Joseph Stuart Hunt, Samuel Leroy Hunt, John Partridge Hunt, James Wilkins Hunt, and Charles Harris Hunt; Continuing to left: Charles Phillip Hunt; Susan Mary Hunt; their daughter Caroline Hunt Nowlin; and James Phillip (Phil) Nowlin, older son of Caroline; In front of Caroline: Stephen Leroy (Lee) Hunt, a nephew of Charles Phillip, and to his right; William Albert (Abe) Nowlin, younger son of Caroline; Seated, left to right: Sallie Stewart Hunt, wife of John Partridge; Edward Franklin (Frank) Haines, older son of Valerie Hunt Haines; daughter Bessie Mary Hunt; daughter Valerie Hunt (Dorothy) Haines; daughter Nellie Susan Hunt Ryder; William Albert Nowlin, husband of Caroline; Ezra Ryder, husband of Nellie. Charles Phillip and Susan Mary Hunt had ten children. Only their oldest child, Lucy Hunt Bierschwale is missing from the photograph.*

*The five sons of Charles Phillip and Susan Mary Hunt. This photograph was cropped out of the foregoing family photograph. Again from left to right, they are, together with their ages at the time: Joe, 24; Sam, 34; Jack, 38; Jim, 42; and Charlie, 44.*

The first of the Hunts to arrive in Arizona was Samuel Leroy (Lee) Hunt, one of C.P.'s nephews. Lee arrived in Bisbee in 1889 and became an underground miner in the copper mines there. He followed that trade for the rest of his working life. James (Jim) was the first of C.P.'s sons to come to Arizona, arriving in Bisbee in 1898. John (Jack) followed in 1900, and the rest arrived in mass in 1902. Two more of C.P.'s nephews, Stewart and David Hunt, had arrived in Arizona a few years before.

Four of C.P.'s five sons, along with cousins Stewart and Dave, entered the cattle ranching business shortly after arriving in Arizona. The one son, that was not in the cattle business, was the oldest, Charles, a medical doctor. See Photo No. 2 of the five sons above. Charles did participate financially with his brothers in some of their ranching ventures. One of the Hunts' early ranches was the Rancho Sacatal in the Sulphur Springs Valley of Southeastern Arizona. The Hunts operated and lived on the Rancho Sacatal until about 1916. During this same period, the Hunts were also involved with Stewart Hunt in his various cattle operations in southeastern Arizona and Northern Mexico.

The Rancho Sacatal was headquartered on 480 acres of deeded land, located about one-half mile north of the Mexican border and about ten miles west of Douglas. The Sulphur Springs Valley is about

30 miles wide, east to west, and it extends north from the international boundary about 30 miles. When the Hunts first took up residence there around 1902 or 1903, the valley was mostly a broad, open expanse of essentially unoccupied government land. Initially, the Hunts and a few others used the valley as open range for their cattle. By 1916, a large number of small farmers or "nesters" had homesteaded and taken up residence in the Sulphur Springs Valley. These newcomers substantially reduced the area and accessibility of the rangeland available to the Hunts for the open grazing of their cattle. The Hunt brothers searched for rangeland better suited to their purposes and settled on the less-developed Animas Valley located in the southwestern corner of New Mexico and about 50 miles east of the Sulphur Springs Valley.

Accordingly, the Hunts left the Rancho Sacatal in 1916 and acquired two homesteads on or near the western side of the Animas Valley. They promptly brought in roughly 1,000 head of cattle from their ranching operations in the Sulphur Springs Valley and Mexico. This large herd of cattle was turned loose to graze in the Animas Valley and nearby grasslands. There were other ranchers already in the area, most notably the Gray Ranch, which was owned by the Kern County Land Company. These existing ranchers did not appreciate the intrusion of the Hunt's large herd onto what was an already fairly crowded rangeland. At about the same time that the Hunts relocated to the Animas Valley, their cousin, Stewart Hunt, acquired a ranch in the nearby Guadalupe Canyon. Stewart also brought a substantial herd of livestock into the area.

Some mention needs to be made here of the general state of land use and ownership in the American Southwest in the early part of the twentieth century. This territory had been acquired by the US from Mexico around 1850. The acquisition came through two treaties, the Guadalupe-Hidalgo and the Gadsden Purchase. The vast majority of the land in Southeastern Arizona and Southwestern New Mexico belonged then and now to the federal government. During the Theodore Roosevelt administration (1901–1908) the higher, wooded areas had generally been designated as US Forest lands. These came under the administration of the US Forest Service under the Department of Agriculture. The Interior Department, through its Bureau of Land Management, was responsible for essentially all of the other federal lands. Through the second half of the 19$^{th}$ century and well into the 20$^{th}$, the federal government made little effort to control the use of its land in the American Southwest. Some small parcels had become private land under the Homestead Act, and the Forest Service had begun to exercise some control through a leasing program. Indeed, the Hunts had acquired a lease on some of the US Forest land adjoining one of their Animas Valley homesteads. With these and a few other exceptions, the Southwest was simply open rangeland, available for use by any and all comers.

This passive attitude on the part of the federal government caused anarchy in the Southwestern rangelands. The desirable grasslands tended to become flooded with grazing cattle. Established ranchers sought to exclude newcomers, and disputes among the competing settlers were common and often violent. Most of the Southwestern rangelands were permanently damaged by overgrazing. Valleys that were once covered with lush grass are now choked with unproductive brush, but that is another story.

There was some cooperation among the competing ranchers, a notable example of which being the regional roundups. The cattle of the various owners in an open area would mix together and range widely. The roundups were conducted once or twice each year for the purpose of inventorying and sorting out the cattle, and for branding the new calves. The practice of branding cattle largely grew out of the need to identify the specific ownership of individual cows gathered in these roundups. Usually, each rancher would either attend or be represented at these gatherings. During the roundups, the ranchers were able to confer and to socialize with their neighbors, and their cowboys had the opportunity to showcase their skills. The modern rodeo may have had its origins here.

The largest and most powerful of the Hunt's adversarial neighbors was the Gray Ranch. This large and long-established cattle ranch was at the time owned by the Kern County Land Company, a wealthy group of investors headquartered in California. The Gray Ranch still exists. It encompasses a major portion of the southern end of New Mexico's Animas Valley. The Gray Ranch brand was then and is now the Diamond A. The foreman of the Gray Ranch in 1917 was William Benjamin (Ben) Robertson.

The primary means of privatizing US Government land in the West was through the Homestead Act of 1862. Some parcels were acquired by private interests as mining claims, and blocks of land were given to the railroads to induce their western expansion. Under the Homestead Act, an individual or family could file for a homestead on a parcel of land containing up to 160 acres. Later versions of the Homestead Act allowed parcels of up to 640 acres. After occupying the homestead for a specified period and making certain qualifying improvements to the land, the individual or family could apply for and obtain a patent or deed to the parcel. The core parcels for the Rancho Sacatal and the parcels, which the Hunts had acquired in and near the Animas Valley, were such homesteads.

As a corporate entity, the Kern County Land Company could not increase its Gray Ranch land holdings by directly acquiring government land under the Homestead Act. To get around this restriction, the owners of the Gray Ranch used a clever, and apparently common, subterfuge. They would first arrange for an individual to apply for a homestead on a parcel of land they wished to acquire. They would then assist the individual in making the improvements required for a patent. Once the individual had obtained the patent, the Kern County Land Company would purchase the parcel at some previously agreed upon price. The individuals, through whom the Gray Ranch acted in acquiring such homesteads, were often the ranch's own cowboys. Chester Bartell may have been one of the individuals with whom the Gray Ranch had such an arrangement. A few months before he was killed, Bartell had filed for a homestead on a parcel near the Gray Ranch. Bartell's homestead was also near one of the Hunt homesteads and adjoined their forest service leasehold.

While Ben Robertson was in charge of the Gray Ranch, he likely made arrangements for these sham homestead transactions. There is some indication that Robertson made the arrangements on behalf of his employers, but then took title to some of the homesteads in his own name. In any event, Robertson later left his employment with the Kern County Land Company under apparently less than amicable circumstances, and then began operating his own cattle ranch nearby. Robertson is even alleged to have acquired other ranch properties in the area by using armed thugs to intimidate and drive off small landholders. Some of his neighbors considered Robertson to be a scoundrel. Whether he deserved this reputation is open to debate, but the Hunts certainly regarded Robertson as a devious enemy, bent on driving them out of the Animas Valley.

Others in the area were also opposed to the Hunts' presence. Principal among these was a rancher named W. H. (Hut) Taylor, the patriarch of an extended family of reputed low-lifes. Hut Taylor was related to Chester Bartell through marriage, and was apparently the de-facto leader of an assorted group of local cattle thieves and troublemakers. Hut Taylor and his cronies were the ones directly involved in the effort to drive the Hunts out of the Animas. In this effort Taylor et al. may not have been acting only in their own interests, since there is a strong suggestion that they also had backing from Ben Robertson and the Kern County Land Company.

The ill will, which the Hunts experienced in the Animas Valley, may have been partly due to their own attitudes. They were morally strait-laced, and their patriarch, Charles P. Hunt, was something of a religious fanatic. Charles P. and his wife Susan were both born in the South before the Civil War to wealthy plantation owners and slaveholders. They had grown up being attended by personal servants, not unlike the character, Scarlet O'Hara, in *Gone with the Wind.* Their wealth and social status largely evaporated in the course of the Civil War; however, they retained some of their antebellum Southern pride, and they imparted it to their children. With considerable sacrifice, the Hunts had even reacquired some social standing by sending two of their sons, Charlie and Sam, to college. It thus seems likely that the prideful Hunts looked upon some of their "coarser" Animas Valley neighbors, particularly the disreputable Hut Taylor clan, with poorly concealed disdain.

Not everyone in the vicinity of the Animas Valley was opposed to the Hunts' presence. The Hunts were somewhat standoffish, but they were honest, hard-working cattlemen, and were on good terms with many of their neighbors. Despite any ill feelings, which Ben Robertson's may have had toward them, the Hunts were friendly with some of the Gray Ranch cowboys.

# The Provocations

In the days and weeks prior to the killing of Chester Bartell, the Hunts were repeatedly harassed by their hostile neighbors. The clear intent of the harassment was to drive the Hunts and their large herd of cattle out of the area. These hostile acts were being carried out by Chester Bartell, Hut Taylor and family, and an assortment of Taylor's cronies, all with the apparent encouragement of the Gray Ranch superintendent, Ben Robertson. As would be learned much later, a substantial financial inducement had been offered for the removal of the Hunts from the Animas Valley.

In their testimony at the trials, the Hunts reported verbal threats and several incidents in which others had come on to the Hunts' Animas Valley ranch property and directed rifle fire at or near them. Some of this gunfire had been aimed at or near the Eldridge Place, where Jack, Sam and Joe lived with their parents and sister. Joe Hunt told of his being shot at on at least two occasions as he rode about the Hunt ranch. On one of these occasions several bullets landed near him while he was saddling a horse at the Blair Place. Joe claimed to have immediately thereafter seen Chester Bartell running away from the area. The Blair Place was an abandoned homestead on the US Forest land, which the Hunts had under lease. Bartell's homestead was only a short distance from the Blair Place.

Another ominous incident occurred while Jack was doing some carpentry work on the house at the Eldridge Place. A man named Lee Howard came by, and noting the work Jack was doing, advised Jack to not to make further improvements to the place since the Hunts would not be living there much longer. Lee Howard's brother, Chap Howard, had been accused by the Hunts of stealing their cattle, and at the time the Hunts were in the process of collecting evidence against Chap Howard. The Howard brothers were relatives of Hut Taylor.

One day during this period, Jim and Jack Hunt discovered and thwarted an attempt by some cowboys to drive a bunch of the Hunt cattle across the international border and into Mexico. As Jim and Jack caught up with them, the cowboys took off, but not before Jack recognized one of them, a man named Tony (Liver-lip) McDonald. Jim and Jack were able to safely return the cattle back to their ranch. Had the cattle been driven over the international border, they would have been quickly seized either by bandits or Mexican authorities. Tony McDonald and the others spotted that day may have been Diamond A cowboys. Although she denied it, Tony McDonald is believed to have been Cora Bartell's cousin and, by marriage, a relative of Hut Taylor.

Apparently, the provocations stopped for a while after Bartell was killed. This interruption in hostile activity may have been the result of a confrontation between Jack Hunt and Ben Robertson. Jack encountered Robertson during the 1917 fall roundup in the Animas Valley. Jack reportedly told Robertson that, if there were any further attempts to harm Jack or his brothers, he (Jack) would personally kill him (Robertson).

# September 13–16, 1917

Chester Bartell was shot and killed September 13, 1917. The following is a brief summary of the events shortly before and after Bartell's demise. These events are more fully described in the recounting of the trial testimony. In reading this and the following sections, readers will probably find it useful to refer to the maps on Pages 6 and 7. Impatient readers may want to have an advance peek at the major turning points and the final outcome of the murder charges. If so, they can refer to the tabulation in "Timeline" on Pages 103 and 104.

On the morning of Thursday, September 13, 1917, three Hunt brothers, Jack, Sam and Joe, were driving a small bunch of their cattle in a northwesterly direction from their ranch headquarters toward another part of their ranch called the Blair Place. They were in the hilly terrain (See Photo No. 7 on Page 24.) at the Eastern edge of the Peloncillo Mountains in the extreme southwestern corner of New Mexico. The broad plain of the Animas Valley lay off to the East.

Around 11:00 AM, the Hunts found Chester Bartell at or near the top of a ridge in rough, brushy country about 1.5 miles from the Eldridge Place, their Animas Valley home. The Hunt brothers and Bartell were all mounted on horses. Shortly before the encounter with Bartell, Jack had ridden off to the left to turn back several cows that

*Looking west at the terrain northwest of the Hunt Ranch house (Eldridge Place) in the Animas Valley. The shooting of Chester Bartell is believed to have occurred in the low hills on the horizon.*

had strayed away from the trail, while Sam and Joe continued on up the trail. Bartell was standing behind a heavy clump of brush, which concealed him from Sam and Joe as they approached him. As they rounded the brush, Sam and Joe spotted Bartell. They believed Bartell was one of the hostile riflemen that had recently fired at or near them. They were undoubtedly correct in this assumption. In any event, Sam and Joe both drew their pistols and shot Bartell dead. Bartell was armed at the time with a rifle, and may have also been carrying a pistol. When confronted by Sam and Joe, Bartell reportedly reached for his rifle, but was unable to get it completely out of its scabbard. The brothers would later claim that they shot Bartell in self-defense. The validity of this claim would be the subject of much debate.

Immediately after the last shot was fired, Jack rejoined his brothers. They were fearful of being ambushed by comrades of Bartell, who might have been lurking close by. For their protection, Jack instructed his two brothers to ride out of the bushy area and into open country, where they could not be ambushed. Jack decided to return to the Eldridge Place and then to report the killing of Bartell to the authorities. Sam and Joe rode out on to the Gray Ranch and into the open terrain of the Animas Valley. They were to stay near the road where Jack could later find them. Bartell's body lay where it had fallen at the time of his death. Bartell's widow, Cora, soon entered the picture.

The Bartells lived on a small homestead four or five miles northwest of the Hunt ranch house. On the morning of September 13, Bartell left home with the avowed intention of paying a friendly visit to the Hunts. He thus rode southeast along the same trail that the Hunts were traveling, but in the opposite direction. When he did not return home as promptly as expected, Mrs. Bartell set out in search of her husband. She followed his horse's tracks until she found his body lying next to the trail. Mrs. Bartell determined that her husband was dead, but without discovering the bullet wounds in his body. She left her husband's body where she found it, and rode on to the Hunt ranch house. She met Jack and other family members at the Hunt house and reported finding her husband's body. Remarkably, the Hunts did not tell her about the shooting. Equally remarkable, Mrs. Bartell spent the night at the Hunt's house.

Shortly after Cora Bartell's appearance at the Hunt ranch house, Jack left by car to find and report the killing of Chester Bartell to the proper authorities. Jack located Louis Carriere, the justice of the peace, near his home in the vicinity of the nearby community of Cloverdale. Jack informed Carriere of the shooting, and Carriere quickly made arrangements for a coroner's inquest. Jack and Carriere then drove together to the Hunt ranch. Along the way they ran into Sam and Joe, waiting alongside the road as previously arranged. Carriere informed Sam and Joe that they were under arrest, but permitted them to ride on home.

The coroner's inquest was held after dark on September 13 at the site of the shooting, where Bartell's body still lay on the ground. The coroner's jury, consisting of Carriere and at least four other men, examined Bartell's body. The jurors later testified to having found only two bullet holes in the body. Following the coroner's inquest, Carriere took the body in one of the Hunts' wagons to the nearby ranch of W. H. (Hut) Taylor. The body was placed on a cot outside the Taylor home at about 4:00 AM on September 14.

At about midnight on September 13, Charles Johnson, constable for the Cloverdale Precinct, came to the Hunt ranch and placed Jack, Sam and Joe under arrest. Apparently the Hunts were not taken into custody. Johnson also spent the night at the Hunt ranch and observed Mrs. Bartell leaving the next morning.

Hut Taylor would later testify that, on the morning of September 14, he observed blood oozing from Bartell's body. He summoned his sons and several neighbors, and together they stripped and examined the body. The participants in this second, unofficial examination of Bartell's body would later testify that they found ten or more bullet wounds in the body. Bartell's body was reportedly buried on Sunday, September 16, 1917.

# The Indictment

On or about March 4, 1918, the Grant County grand jury indicted Jack, Sam and Joe Hunt on first-degree murder charges for the killing of Chester Bartell. The trial date was set for March 21, 1918 in the District Court for the Sixth Judicial District in Silver City, New Mexico.

At the time of the indictment, all three of the Hunt brothers were at liberty on bail of $25,000 each or a total of $75,000. For bail to have been set, there must have been a preliminary hearing beforehand. The record is unclear, but it appears that the preliminary hearing was held on or about November 14, 1917. In 1917–18, $75,000 was a whopping sum. The modern day equivalent would be about 13 times that amount or about $1,000,000. The Hunts did not have assets of this magnitude, but they evidently had some wealthy benefactors, who guaranteed their bail bonds. These benefactors are believed to have included Lemuel Shattuck and members of the Greenway family. Shattuck was a banker in Bisbee Arizona with wide interests in mining and cattle ranching. The Greenways, also of Bisbee, were large stockholders in the Calumet and Arizona Mining Company, and they were closely involved in the management of that copper mining company.

On March 6, 1918, a formal warrant for the arrest of the Jack, Sam and Joe Hunt was signed by district judge, Raymond R. Ryan. The Grant County sheriff, W. F. Shriver, served the warrant on the three defendants on March 11, 1918 in Silver City. The warrant was read to the defendants, but already being under bond, they were not taken into physical custody.

According to the district court records, five witnesses were subpoenaed to testify before the grand jury. A total of about forty witnesses were subpoenaed to testify at the trial. Ben Robertson was one of those forty or so witnesses. There is no record of Robertson actually testifying.

At the time of the killing of Chester Bartell and for over a year thereafter, the United States was engaged in World War I. Joe Hunt was 22 years old in 1917, and in August, he had volunteered for service in the US Army. He was waiting to be called to service in the Army on September 13, when Bartell was killed. The killing of Bartell and subsequent murder charges precluded Joe's being called up by the Army.

# The First Trial

The Sixth Judicial District court in Silver City, New Mexico had a crowded docket in the spring term of 1918, and the Hunt Brothers' trial (Case No. 7015) did not actually begin until Monday, April 1, 1918. The trial would end the following Monday when the jury announced its verdict. Most of what we know of this trial comes from the verbatim record of the witness' testimony. Also useful to us was a remarkably detailed newspaper article published in the *Silver City Independent* on April 9, 1918. A transcript of the article is included herewith as Appendix B.

Local interest in the trial was very high. The newspapers reported that a great many spectators attended the trial. Many years later, Joseph P. Hunt, my brother and the son of Joseph S. Hunt, talked to a man, who stated that he had been in Silver City at the time of the trial. This individual reported witnessing a confrontation on a Silver City street between Joe and several men, who were taunting him, and that, "Joe Hunt put the fear of God in those fellas." The truth of this man's account may be questionable, but the tension around the courthouse in Silver City during the trial must have been palpable.

On top of the expense of sustaining the large bail bonds, the Hunts had engaged a sizable, and no doubt costly, team of defense lawyers. The chief defense counsel was Clifton Mathews of Bisbee.

He was assisted by one of his partners, John M. Ross, and three lawyers from the Silver City area. The local lawyers were James S. Casey of Tyrone and Percy Wilson and Joseph F. Woodbury of Silver City. District Attorney J. S. Vaught conducted the prosecution with the assistance of two special prosecutors, C. C. Royall and K. K. Scott. Royall was described as the special prosecutor for Mrs. Bartell. Presiding at the trial was District Judge Raymond R. Ryan.

The intense local interest and publicity about the case apparently caused the attorneys for both sides to be selective in picking the jury. Twelve individuals, all men and all having Anglo names, were finally chosen. Jury selection occupied the first two days of the trial.

## The Prosecution

Presentation of evidence began when the court session opened on Wednesday morning.

Mrs. Cora Bartell was the first witness for the prosecution. Her testimony contained the expected tear-jerking elements. She recounted her and her husband's movements in the several years prior to his death. Since their marriage in 1914, they had lived in several locations in Southeastern Arizona, mostly on ranches belonging to Mrs. Bartell's family, the McDonalds. The Bartells purchased and settled on a homestead just north of the Blair Place in August 1913.

Cora Bartell testified that her husband had left their homestead on the morning of September 13,1917 with the intention of visiting the Hunts. The Bartell homestead was located about five miles northwest of the Hunt ranch headquarters. Bartell had been unsuccessful in developing a well on his homestead, and reportedly told his wife that he was going to see the Hunts in hopes of arranging with them for watering his cattle at the Blair Place. Reportedly, he had even taken a puppy with him as a gift to the Hunts. The Bartells' two-year-old child was ill, and Mrs. Bartell wanted to take the child to a doctor in Douglas. Accordingly, she had asked her husband to return home from his visit to the Hunts as quickly as possible.

Chester Bartell did not return home promptly, and Cora Bartell reported that the puppy returned home alone. Mrs. Bartell then set out on horseback to find her husband. She took her sick child along. The direction her husband was to have ridden, toward the Hunt ranch house, was also the direction they would have traveled in going to Douglas. The ground was wet from a recent rainstorm, and Mrs. Bartell was able to easily follow the tracks of her husband's horse. Cora told of her infant son being the first to notice his father lying on the ground, and she recounted her shock and grief at finding that her husband was dead. She also found his horse nearby, with Bartell's 30-30 rifle still in the scabbard tied to the saddle. Although she determined that her husband was dead, Mrs. Bartell apparently did not notice any bullet wounds in his body. She stated that she assumed that he had died accidentally, possibly having fallen from his horse and then been dragged to death.

Mrs. Bartell reported taking the rifle out of the scabbard on her husband's horse and leaving the horse near her husband's body. She then left her husband's body where she found it, and rode rapidly on to the Hunt ranch house, arriving around 2:00 PM. She met Jack, his sister, Bess, and their parents at the house and reported to them the finding of her husband's body. Inexplicably, Jack did not tell Mrs. Bartell how her husband had died. She testified that, upon her arrival there, she saw Jack Hunt outside the house wearing a carpenter's apron and carrying a hammer. She asked Jack to assist her in retrieving her husband's body, but reported that Jack only responded by saying that he would go get the deputy sheriff, and promptly thereafter left in his automobile. Remarkably, Mrs. Bartell and her child spent the night at the Hunts' house.

Cora Bartell stated that she did not learn that her husband had been shot until the following morning, September 14. She left the Hunt Ranch and went to the nearby Hut Taylor ranch on the morning of September 14 in the company of Hut Taylor's sons, Marion and Lee Taylor. Hut Taylor was married to the sister of Cora Bartell's mother. In the course of her testimony, Mrs. Bartell identified the shoes, overalls and shirt, which her husband had been wearing at the time of his death.

The next witness was Hut Taylor. He told of Judge Carriere's delivering Bartell's body to his ranch house early in the morning on September 14. He also stated that he suspected that Carriere had understated the number of wounds in Bartell's body, and that he called in more than a dozen of his neighbors to witness another examination of the body. He gave detailed descriptions of the bullet wounds, which he, his sons and his neighbors reportedly found when they stripped and examined the body. According to Hut Taylor, he and his team found a total of ten wounds in Bartell's body located as follows:

- One in the left breast entering just under the nipple and exiting through the back near the right shoulder blade;
- One through the left arm near the elbow;
- One at the point of the left shoulder;
- One in the right knee;
- Two in the left thigh;
- Three in the right hip, close together;
- And one through the right foot at the big toe.

Taylor testified that some of these wounds were still oozing blood on the morning of September 14. Taylor also stated that Bartell's backbone and the hips were all "broken to pieces, " and the left leg was shattered. He further stated that the body could be easily twisted at the points of these bone breaks. In the course of their unofficial examination, Hut Taylor et al. undressed and washed Bartell's body. It remained in Taylor's barn until the body was placed in a coffin and taken away on the morning of September 15 by Bill McDonald and Henry Eicks. Bill McDonald was Cora Bartell's uncle and Henry Eicks was her brother-in-law. McDonald and Eicks were thus also both relatives, by marriage, of Hut Taylor himself.

Taylor was shown the previously introduced items of Bartell's clothing, and he correlated the location of some of the wounds in the body with holes and bloodstains on the clothing. Under cross-examination, Taylor admitted that he and one of his sons were the only ones who had access to the body for two or more hours after its arrival at his ranch on September 14.

Taylor also related how he and Tobe Lacey had visited the scene of the killing on September 15, where they found a large bloodstain on the ground near the trail. He described the physical features of the area, and stated that he was familiar with the area because he had once owned the Eldridge Place. He reported finding six empty "cartridge hulls" from a 45-caliber automatic pistol within about 20 feet of the bloodstain. He produced the empty cartridges, and they were entered in evidence.

Tobe Lacey next testified and confirmed Hut Taylor's account of the bullet wounds in Bartell's body. Lacey also told of accompanying Hut Taylor to the scene of the shooting on September 15. Under cross-examination, Lacey admitted that he had recently served time in the Arizona state prison at Yuma after being convicted of stealing cattle. Other witnesses, who were present during the examination of the body at the Taylor ranch, corroborated the testimony of Taylor and Lacey about the bullet wounds. These other witnesses included James Morehead, William Birchfield, Joe Yarbro and E. W. (Rat) Taylor, another of Hut Taylor's sons.

The next witness was Justice of the Peace Louis Carriere. He told of Jack Hunt locating him on the afternoon of September 13 near Cloverdale and Jack's reporting the killing of Chester Bartell by Sam and Joe Hunt. Carriere accompanied Jack back up the valley in Jack's car. They ran into Sam and Joe Hunt waiting on their horses alongside the road. Carriere placed Sam and Joe under arrest, and then released them upon receiving their promise to return home and wait.

Jack and Carriere then proceeded to the Gray Ranch headquarters, where Carriere recruited men to serve on a coroner's jury. They then went to the Hunt ranch, and then on to the scene of the killing, arriving about 8:00 PM. Bartell's body was still lying on the ground where he had fallen after being shot. Carriere and his coroner's jury conducted their examination of the body, where it lay. As a prosecution witness, Carriere was not asked and did not reveal the specific findings of the coroner's inquest. These details would come out later in the trial.

Jack Simms, a cowboy for the Gray Ranch, testified that he had seen and visited with Sam and Joe Hunt about 1:00 PM on the afternoon of September 13. This meeting had taken place at the Fitzpatrick, a corral and watering place on the Gray Ranch. The Fitzpatrick was about seven miles south and east of the Hunts' home at the Eldridge Place. According to Simms, Sam and Joe did not mention anything about Bartell in the conversation at the Fitzpatrick. Simms did testify that he was later recruited by Judge Carriere to serve on the coroner's jury, and that he had accompanied Jack and Carriere as they drove back up the Animas Valley to the Hunt ranch.

At the conclusion of Simms' testimony for the prosecution, the district attorney unexpectedly moved that the court instruct the jury to acquit Jack Hunt. In making this motion, the district attorney stated that there was insufficient evidence against Jack to warrant his prosecution. The court accepted the motion. Jack Hunt was acquitted and discharged, and was immediately thereafter placed on the stand as a prosecution witness.

Jack recounted the events of September 13, 1917 as he had witnessed them. I had a lot of contact with Jack Hunt while I was growing up. I knew him to be scrupulously honest. He was certainly not sympathetic to the prosecution, but I feel quite certain that his testimony would have been accurate. Jack related that, on the morning of September 13, 1917, he and his brothers, Sam and Joe, had gathered a herd of ten to fifteen head of cattle around the Eldridge Place. The water at the Eldridge Place was drying up, and they intended to relocate the cattle to a watering place about one and three-quarters miles away to the northwest. Between 10:00 and 11:00 AM, they began driving the herd of cattle along the trail leading to the Blair Place. All were riding cow horses.

As they neared the top of a ridge, Jack stated that several cows had strayed off the trail to the left. Jack rode out a short distance away from his brothers to bring the strays back to the trail. While so engaged, he recalled being startled at hearing several shots in quick succession. He was unable to say how many shots he had heard. He galloped quickly to the scene of the shooting, believing that his brothers had been ambushed. There, he found his brothers still holding their pistols and saw Bartell lying on the ground near the trail, apparently dead. The three brothers decided to leave the scene of the shooting as quickly as possible, in the belief that other hostile parties could have also been lurking about the rough, bushy area waiting to ambush them.

The encounter with and shooting of Bartell took place about a mile and a quarter from the Eldridge Place. Jack instructed Sam and Joe to ride east into an open part of the Animas Valley and out onto the Gray Ranch property. Jack returned to the Hunt ranch house with the avowed intention of finding and reporting the shooting of Bartell to the appropriate authorities.

At the conclusion of Jack's testimony, the state rested its case. The defense moved for a directed verdict of acquittal for both Sam and Joe. The motion was denied.

## The Defense

The defense began its presentation after the lunch recess on Thursday. At that time, Justice of the Peace Carriere was recalled to the witness stand. He told of swearing in the coroner's jury and then conducting a coroner's inquest at the scene of the shooting. In addition to himself, the coroner's jury consisted of six men, all of whom were employed by Gray Ranch. He stated that he and the other jurors had fully stripped Bartell's body and had then made a complete and careful examination of the body. Carriere reported finding only two bullet wounds. One was from a bullet entering the left chest below the nipple and exiting below the right shoulder blade, and the other, a flesh wound in the right thigh. He also reported finding a 45- caliber bullet, an empty 45-caliber cartridge and a water bottle near the body. He testified that the body was rigidly stiff and that there was no indication of any broken bones. He said that the left shoe was off the dead man's foot.

After completing the inquest, Carriere went with Jack Hunt in Jack's car to find the deputy sheriff, Charlie Johnson. In the meantime, the body remained in the custody of other members of the coroner's jury. A wagon was obtained and the body loaded on to it. After finding and returning with Johnson, Carriere took charge of the wagon and delivered Bartell's body to the home of W. H. (Hut) Taylor. He dropped off the body and turned it over to the custody of Taylor sometime after midnight on September 14.

Carriere was subjected to an intense cross-examination by the prosecution. The district attorney asserted that, in an earlier interview,

Carriere had told the district attorney and others that he (Carriere) had not carefully examined Bartell's body and that the inquest had taken place after dark with only a smoky lantern and a flashlight for illumination. Carriere confirmed that the inquest had taken place after dark, but steadfastly denied that the lighting had been poor, or that Bartell's body had not been given a careful and thorough examination by the coroner's jury.

The defense subsequently called four other members of the coroner's jury to the stand. They were Jack Simms, Bert Rhodes, George Parish and Munro Dunnegan. All four of these witnesses stated that they had found only two bullet wounds in Bartell's body and otherwise corroborated Carriere's testimony. On cross-examination, Rhodes did admit to being a friend of the Hunts. Simms spent the night of September 13 at the Hunt ranch. He reported seeing Cora Bartell carrying a pistol when she left the next morning.

Elizabeth (Bess) Hunt, the Hunt Brothers' sister, testified about Mrs. Bartell coming to the Hunt ranch house on September 13. Bess stated that Mrs. Bartell had told her of finding Bartell's horse near the scene of the killing, and of finding Bartell's Winchester rifle partly out of its scabbard.

Charles Johnson, the deputy sheriff and constable for the Cloverdale District, testified as to his having gone to the Hunt ranch, arriving around midnight on September 13. He stated that he then placed Jack, Sam and Joe under arrest. Johnson stayed overnight at the Hunt ranch. He reported having observed Mrs. Bartell the following morning, as she was leaving the Hunt ranch. Johnson said that Mrs. Bartell was then carrying a six-shooter wrapped in a web belt, and that she had handed the pistol to one of the Taylors.

Next came expert testimony by O. J. Westlake, a medical doctor. He testified that rigor mortis would have fully set in a few hours after

Bartell's death, and that the resulting stiffness would have later made it difficult to manipulate and undress Bartell's body. He indicated that, after rigor mortis had set in, it would be difficult to manipulate the body even where bones had been broken.

Dr. Westlake also stated that a body would cease to bleed profusely shortly after death had occurred. He further indicated that "serum" could ooze from wounds inflicted many hours after death. Serum was vaguely defined as a body fluid somewhat like blood, but thinner. The testimony of Dr. Westlake was apparently offered to bring in to question the testimony of Hut Taylor and his unofficial coroner's jury. On cross-examination by the prosecution, the witness was asked to examine bloodstains on Bartell's clothing. Dr. Westlake opined that some of the bloodstains on the victim's clothing would have been from bleeding before or soon after death. He also noted that other areas of the clothing were stained with serum—not blood. The prosecution was apparently trying to establish that holes in the clothing had been from bullets entering the body at or near the time of Bartell's death. In reading Dr. Westlake's testimony, it seems that it would have been somewhat contradictory to a jury of laymen.

Jack Hunt was again called to the witness stand. Jack's testimony as a defense witness was consistent with his previous testimony, but more extensive and detailed. Under direct examination by the defense attorneys, Jack provided a lot of background information on himself and his family. At the time of the trial (April 1918), Jack was 36 years old. He stated that he had been born and raised in Texas, and had lived in Arizona since 1900. For the first six years after arriving in Arizona, Jack had worked in the mines in Bisbee. He had then lived and worked for about eight years on the family's ranch in the Sulphur Springs Valley in Southeastern Arizona. Jack came to the Animas Valley in May or June 1917. For the three years prior to that, Jack had managed a family-owned farm near Yuma, Arizona.

Since coming to the Animas Valley, Jack had lived with his brothers, Sam and Joe, and their parents and sister, Bess, on the Eldridge Place. At the time, Jack, Sam, Joe and Bess were all unmarried. The Eldridge Place was a 160-acre homestead on which Sam had filed. There was a small, two-room house on the Eldridge Place. Jack had added screened porches on the front and back sides of the house. The Eldridge Place adjoined a US Forest lease held by the Hunt brothers. The Blair Place was part of their US Forest lease. Apparently the Blair Place was an abandoned homestead located about four miles north and west of the Eldridge Place. The extent of the forest lease was vaguely stated as being about four miles by five miles. Joe also spent part of his time on a homestead, which he had filed on. Joe's homestead was about five miles south and west of the Eldridge Place and was located at or near the head of Cloverdale Creek.

Jack stated that he and his four brothers were all jointly involved in their cattle ranching operations. Jack, Sam and Joe handled the day-to-day operation of their ranch properties. They had no other employees. Jim lived in Douglas and looked after the business side of things. Charlie, the medical doctor, lived in Bisbee and had only a financial involvement in the ranches. In September 1917, the Hunts had about 1,000 head of cattle in the Animas Valley. At the time of trial (April 1918) the herd had been reduced to about 200 head.

Jack told of his brother having been shot at, and of hostile gunfire being directed at the Hunt home, a few days before they encountered and shot Bartell. They had reported these incidents to Deputy Sheriff Johnson and he had advised them to arm themselves for protection. They also consulted with Harry Wheeler, the sheriff of Cochise County, Arizona, and received the same advice. Accordingly, Jack and both his brothers were all carrying loaded rifles and pistols when they rode away from home on the morning of September 13.

After the shooting of Bartell, Jack separated from his brothers and rode back home, arriving about noon. He unsaddled and released his horse. As he was walking toward the house, Jack spotted two men on horseback disappearing into some nearby bushes. He recognized one them as Lee Taylor, a son of Hut Taylor, and the other as Tony (Liver Lip) McDonald, another of Hut Taylor's associates. Jack stayed around outside the house watching for these hostile individuals for what he estimated to be a half hour. Bess then called him into lunch and he went into the house. He stated that he did not at that time tell his sister or parents about the shooting of Bartell. He had a small bit of lunch and went back outside, just as Cora Bartell rode up. Mrs. Bartell told him of finding her husband's body and asked Jack for his assistance in bringing in the body. Jack didn't tell Mrs. Bartell about the shooting either. Instead, he told her that the body should be first examined by the authorities. He then got into his car and set off for the community of Cloverdale. Under cross-examination, Jack denied that he was wearing a carpenter's apron and carrying a hammer when Mrs. Bartell arrived at the Eldridge Place.

In the evening of September 13, Jack accompanied Judge Carriere and members of the coroner's jury to the site of the shooting. He then stood by while the coroner's jury examined Bartell's body. Jack confirmed that the coroner's jury had fully stripped and exposed the body, and Jack swore that he too had only seen two wounds in the body. Thereafter, he and Carriere went off in Jack's car in search of Deputy Sheriff Johnson. After finding Johnson, Jack brought him and Carriere back to the Hunt ranch. Jack had a busy day on September 13. The prosecution cross-examined Jack at great length. Jack stuck to his story, but the prosecutor was successful in exposing Jack's somewhat odd behavior in the few hours after the shooting.

Sam Hunt was the next witness. At the time of the trial, Sam was 32 years old and single. He told of his having been born and raised in

Texas. After arriving in Arizona in 1902 at the age of 17, he lived with the family on their ranch in the Sulphur Springs Valley. He worked for about six years in the mines in Bisbee and also attended school. He later spent some time on the Hunt family farm in Yuma. Sam came to the Animas Valley in August 1916, at which time he filed on and took possession of a 160-acre homestead, the Eldridge Place. Sam lived at the Eldridge place with his parents; his brothers, Jack and Joe; and his sister, Bess.

Sam's recounting of events on September 13, 1917 agreed closely with the testimony of his brother, Jack. He told of several cows straying off the trail as they were moving the cows to the new watering place on the morning of September 13. After Jack had ridden off to the left to retrieve the strays, Sam said that he rode uphill a short distance to a point where the trail forked around a large piñon tree. The piñon tree together with some underbrush formed a dense barrier. Accordingly, a rider approaching the fork from the direction Sam was riding would have been unable to see beyond the piñon tree. Sam took the left fork around the piñon, and Joe went around to the right. As he rounded the tree Sam was shocked to see Bartell sitting on his horse close to the trail and only about 30 feet away. Bartell was looking directly at Sam and was leaning back, reaching down to the right and attempting to withdraw his Winchester from its scabbard. Seeing this, Sam drew his pistol and began firing at Bartell, and continued firing until Bartell fell from his horse. The firing only lasted a few seconds and neither Sam, Joe or Bartell said a word before or during the shooting. Joe began firing shortly after Sam fired his first shot. Sam related that, as he was falling, Bartell's left foot momentarily hung in the stirrup. The left shoe pulled off Bartell's foot and he then fell off the right side of his horse. Sam claimed that he fired only five times. His pistol was a conventional, frontier-type six-gun. Sam said that he believed that, in reaching for his rifle, Bartell intended to kill him and that he shot at

Bartell in self-defense. He emphatically denied having shot at Bartell after he had fallen from his horse. Sam did not know whether it was he or Joe who had fatally wounded Bartell

Sam was questioned at length about the physical details of the shooting scene. He claimed to be well acquainted with the area, because he rode through it almost every day in going back and forth from home to the Blair Place. The defense team had hired a professional photographer named Mason, and he had taken photos at and around the shooting scene from various positions and directions. The photos were introduced into evidence, while Sam was on the witness stand. The descriptions of the shooting scene given by Sam and his brothers differed from the descriptions by Hut Taylor and several other prosecution witnesses. If there was any significance in these discrepancies, it is unclear.

When Sam and Joe encountered Bartell, he was sitting on his horse on the trail and near the top of a ridge. Under prodding from the prosecution Sam estimated that Bartell, had he been in that same position, could possibly have seen the Hunts coming as they topped another ridge about one-half mile away. He also added that because of the trees, bush and rough terrain, that Bartell would have only been able to see the Hunts intermittently as they came closer. There was, of course, no way of knowing how long Bartell had been waiting at or near the location where he was shot.

Sam told of riding out with Joe into the open part of the Animas Valley after the shooting. He also told of meeting and conversing with Jack Simms at the Fitzpatrick that afternoon In their conversation with Simms, he and Joe did not mention the shooting of Bartell. Sam also told of he and Joe meeting Jack, Carriere and Jack Simms as they drove along the road in Jack's car. Sam and Joe then rode on home, arriving there about sundown. That evening Sam accompanied Jack and the coroner's jury to the scene of the shooting. He, too, said that he saw only two bullet wounds in Bartell's body. Sam later brought up two mules and a wagon for use by Carriere et al. in transporting the body away from the scene of the shooting.

Joe Hunt was the next defense witness. He told of coming to the Animas Valley in August of 1916. Like his brothers, he came to the Animas from their ranch in the Sulphur Springs Valley in Cochise County, Arizona. At the time of the trial, Joe was 22 years old. Upon arriving in the Animas he had purchased an existing homestead at the upper end of Cloverdale Creek. He divided his time between that homestead and the Eldridge Place, where Sam, Jack, Bess and their parents lived. A family named Good (Goode?) also lived at Joe's homestead. Joe did most of the range riding in tending to the Hunt cattle. The cow horses ridden by he and his brothers were kept at the Blair place, and Joe went back and forth between the Blair Place and the Eldridge Place almost daily.

Joe told of two rifle shots coming close to him while near the Blair Place on September 7, 1917. When this rifle fire was directed at him, Joe was riding past a homestead belonging to a man named Barnet. Joe didn't see Bartell on this occasion, but saw his horse tied to the hitching rail at Barnet's homestead. On the following day, September 8, Joe said that he was saddling a horse at the Blair Place when two more rifle bullets came close to him. Joe rode quickly in the direction from which the shots had come, and saw Bartell fleeing over the ridge toward his homestead. Joe said that he recognized Bartell by the clothes he was wearing. He also said that Bartell was carrying a rifle as he ran toward his home. Joe stated that on September 9 and 10, rifle fire was directed at the Hunt ranch house. These incidents were reported to Deputy Sheriff Johnson, and he advised the Hunts to arm themselves. Jack, Sam and Joe took Johnson's advice and were all armed with pistols and rifles when riding along the trail toward the Blair Place on September 13. Joe said that some of the Hunt cattle had been stolen recently, and that they believed that Bartell was probably one of the cow thieves. The Hunts were in the process of collecting specific evidence against Chap Howard, a known cattle rustler and another of Hut Taylor's relatives.

Joe's account of the actual shooting and their subsequent movements on September 13 agreed very closely with his brothers' versions of the events. Joe began firing at Bartell after hearing Sam's first shot. He testified that he fired only three rounds from his pistol, and that all three rounds were fired while he was some 25 or 30 feet from Bartell. Joe was armed with a .45 caliber automatic. Unlike the revolver that Sam was carrying, an automatic pistol ejects the empty cartridge each time it is fired. Joe also claimed to have stopped firing as soon as Bartell began falling from his horse, and Joe strongly denied having shot at Bartell after he fell to the ground. Under cross-examination Joe was asked to explain how it was that, at the shooting scene, Judge Carriere had found one empty cartridge and a bullet near Bartell's body, and that Hut Taylor and Tobe Lacey had found another six empty cartridges near the bloodstain. Joe could not explain why the cartridge found by Carriere was near the body, but Joe asserted that Taylor and Lacey had lied about finding the six cartridges in an effort to "frame" the Hunts. Joe claimed that he shot at Bartell in self-defense after noting that Bartell was reaching for his Winchester, and believing that Bartell intended to kill both he and Sam. Joe estimated that the shooting had occurred between 10:00 and 11:00 AM.

The defense closed its case by calling several character witnesses. These included J.E. Brophy and M.E. Cassidy of Bisbee, William Riggs of Douglas, William Birchfield and Holmes Maddox of Animas, John E. Evans of Tyrone, and Charles Johnson (the deputy sheriff/constable) of Cloverdale. It is interesting to note that Birchfield had already testified for the prosecution as one of the neighbors who had observed Hut Taylor's examination of Bartell's body on the morning of September 14. The character witnesses all attested to the good character of the Hunt brothers and asserted that they were held in high esteem both by their neighbors in the Animas Valley and by the residents of the Arizona communities where they had previously lived and worked. The defense closed on Friday afternoon, and the prosecution immediately began offering the testimony of rebuttal witnesses.

## Rebuttal

An undertaker and embalmer, named S. Ernest Pollock, was called as a rebuttal witness by the state. He gave expert testimony on rigor mortis and its effect on a dead body. He said that, while a body was stiff from rigor mortis, it could still be readily manipulated at points where the neck or other bones were broken. This contradicted part of Dr. Westlake's testimony. Otherwise, Pollock's testimony seemed largely inconclusive.

District Attorney Vaught took the stand personally in an effort to refute the testimony of Justice of the Peace Carriere. Vaught claimed that Carriere had stated to him and others, during an interview in February 1918, that the coroner's jury had made only a cursory examination of Bartell's body and that the examination of the body had taken place under poor lighting conditions. Vaught's testimony was corroborated by Deputy Sheriff Jesse Cook, who was also present at the interview with Carriere in February. Miss Francis Nutt, the grand jury stenographer, was called as a witness. She stated that, during the grand jury hearing, Jack Simms had said the only illumination during the coroner's inquest had been an "old lantern."

Cora Bartell was recalled to the witness stand. She testified that on September 7, 8, 9 and 10, 1917 her husband spent most of the time digging a well on their homestead. She further stated that she had been with her husband continuously on those dates. This testimony was intended to refute Joe Hunt's testimony that Bartell had shot at him on September 7 and 8 and had possibly shot at the Hunt ranch house on September 9 and 10 as well. Mrs. Bartell also testified that, at the urging of the district attorney, she had returned to the site of the killing on March 15, 1918. She reported being accompanied during that visit to the site by her uncle, Davis McDonald and a Mr. Black. This trio, according to Mrs. Bartell, had dug around the scene of the killing and had uncovered a steel jacketed bullet near where her husband's body had lain. They had found the bullet a few inches below the rocky ground surface, and it had been flattened from striking a rock.

The location and flattening of the bullet indicated that it had traveled vertically downward. If this bullet had been fired by the Hunts at the time of Bartell' demise, its apparently vertical trajectory would seem to contradict part of the defendants' testimony. Sam and Joe Hunt had both stated that they had fired at Bartell, only while both he and they had been sitting on their horses. If this were true, then the bullets fired from the Hunts' pistols would have all traveled more or less horizontally.

Marion Taylor then testified that he had visited the Bartell homestead on September 15, 1917. While there he reported seeing Bartell's six-shooter in a scabbard on a belt wrapped around the head of the bedstead. This evidence by Marion Taylor was apparently intended to support Mrs. Bartell's contention that she was not carrying the pistol on the morning of September 14. Jake New corroborated Marion Taylor's testimony. The final rebuttal witness was Davis McDonald, who corroborated Mrs. Bartell's testimony about finding the bullet on March 15, 1918 at the scene of the killing.

McDonald had the bullet in his possession and it was introduced in evidence over the objection of the defense. After McDonald's testimony ended, the prosecution again closed its case. It was then late Friday evening.

## The Closing Arguments

The closing arguments began when the court reconvened at 9:00 o'clock on Saturday morning. They lasted all day and into the evening. Closing arguments were presented by six different attorneys. Charles C. Royall, the special prosecutor for Mrs. Bartell, spoke first. He was followed by James S. Casey, who spoke for the defense. K. K. Scott, the assistant prosecutor, was the next to address the jury. Percy Wilson then presented his version of the defense case.

Clifton Mathews, the lead attorney for the defense, then presented the final, closing argument for the defense. Mr. Mathews was particularly loquacious. He spoke for four hours and twenty minutes. Unlike the testimony of witnesses, the closing arguments were not recorded verbatim. We do know, however, that Mr. Mathews made a particular effort to convince the jury that Hut Taylor or his sons had inflicted additional wounds in Bartell's body after the body had been delivered to Taylor's ranch. Mathews contended that this had been done by the Taylors to make it appear that the Hunts had continued to fire at Bartell after he had fallen to the ground.

That Sam and Joe Hunt had shot and killed Bartell was not in question. It is clear that the crux of these long-winded arguments was whether or not Sam and Joe, in killing Bartell, had acted in self-defense or had murdered him in anger. The critical physical evidence was in the number and nature of the bullet wounds in Bartell's body. It would be consistent with their claim of self defense, for the Hunts to have inflicted only the two bullet wounds as attested to by Justice of the Peace Carriere and others on the coroner's jury. If on the other hand, the Hunts had shot Bartell ten or more times as indicated by the testimony of Hut Taylor and his comrades, then it would appear that the Hunts had acted in an angry and willful manner. The evidence of the bullet later found at the scene of the killing by Cora Bartell and her uncle was also pertinent. Of particular interest was the bullet wound to Bartell's right foot. The bullet had entered the shoe through the sole near the toe. The shoe had been entered into evidence, in the course of Mrs. Bartell's testimony.

Based on the testimony of Hut Taylor and his friends, the prosecution argued that Sam and Joe Hunt had fired far more shots at Bartell than needed for self-defense and accordingly, had murdered him. In particular, the bullet hole in Bartell's shoe was, according to the prosecution, a clear indication that the Hunts had continued to fire at Bartell after he had fallen to the ground. The defense countered that the Hunts, when confronted by an armed and hostile adversary, had acted only in self-defense, and that the Hunts had shot Bartell only twice, as shown by the testimony of the respected justice of the peace and his coroner's jury. The defense claimed that the additional bullet wounds in Bartell's body had been inflicted much later by the Taylors or others in an effort to incriminate the Hunts. This defense position was to some extent supported by Dr. Westlake's testimony, particularly his assertion that bullet wounds would not bleed if the wounds were inflicted twelve or more hours after death.

When Mr. Mathews had completed his address to the jury, the judge called a recess, and a subtle, but significant, sequence of events took place. Upon the recess being called, the defendants and their attorneys immediately left the courtroom. The judge and some of the jurors, however, were still in the courtroom. While the defendants were thus absent, a juror, M. N. Ross, spoke up and told the judge that the jury wanted Bartell's right shoe cut open to see if there were any traces of blood inside it. The judge responded by saying that any such request by the jury would have to be made in open court. This brief exchange was overheard by the district attorney and several bystanders.

When the court reconvened after the recess, District Attorney J. H. Vaught presented the last prosecution argument. At this juncture and in open court, the juror Ross rose and again requested that the victim's shoe be cut open. The defense was not then aware of the previous exchange between Ross and the judge, and hearing Ross' request took the defense team by surprise. On the other hand, the judge and the prosecution both had foreknowledge of the jury's curiosity about the shoe's interior. Both the prosecution and the defense, in some disarray, assented to juror's request. Under the direction of the court, the sheriff cut the shoe open. The interior of Bartell's right shoe had not previously been visible, but was now fully exposed. Around and near the bullet hole there was what appeared to be a considerable amount of dried blood. The now-open shoe was passed around the jury for their inspection.

The judge then read his detailed instructions to the jury. The instructions were lengthy, running to some twenty-seven typed-written pages. We found a copy of the instructions in the court files. They defined and explained such things as first and second-degree murder, manslaughter, premeditation, criminal intent and self-defense. Delivery of the instructions took almost an hour, after which the court recessed. It was then almost 11:00 PM. The jurors, who must have now been bleary-eyed, then retired to begin their deliberations. In his instructions, the judge gave the jury three options. They could find either or both defendants guilty of first-degree murder, guilty of second-degree murder or innocent by reason of self-defense.

After the jury had retired, the judge informed the defense of the conversation between the judge and juror Ross, which conversation had taken place in the absence of the defendants and their counsel. Only then did the defense learn of this exchange between Ross and the judge. A written statement, apparently prepared by the judge himself and describing the conversation in detail, was entered in the trial record. The defense then contended that the conversation, between the judge and the juror outside the knowledge of the defense, served to deny the defendants a fair and impartial trial. Accordingly, the defense moved that a mistrial be declared and the jury dismissed. The motion was denied.

## The Verdict And Sentence

As is often the case in criminal trials, the jury was faced with two persuasive, but conflicting, versions of the events surrounding the killing of Chester Bartell.

Did the coroner's jury really find only two bullet wounds? Was their inspection of the body slipshod and done under poor lighting conditions? Was Carriere in league with the Hunts, and did he and Jack Hunt concoct the idea of minimizing the number of bullet wounds? If so, how did they get the other members of the coroner's jury to go along? How did the coroner's jury miss the obvious wound in Bartell's right foot? The physical descriptions of the shooting scene given by the prosecution witnesses varied significantly from that provided by the Hunts. What was the significance of that?

Had Bartell been shooting at Joe Hunt prior to September 13? If so, how did Joe Hunt really know that Bartell was the assailant? Why was Bartell carrying a rifle, and maybe a pistol, if he was visiting the Hunt ranch with only peaceful intentions? The Hunts were driving a herd of cattle, and Bartell must surely have been aware of their presence before they reached and confronted him. Did Bartell have his pistol with him? Was Bartell lying in wait to ambush the Hunts?

If so and if he was carrying a pistol, why didn't he attempt to use the pistol instead of the more cumbersome rifle?

What about the Taylors? They were relatives and obviously friends of Bartell and his wife. It must have been clear to the jury that the Taylors, Bartell and possibly others had conspired against the Hunts. Did the Taylors inflict additional wounds in Bartell's lifeless body to incriminate the Hunts? Were they that clever? Taylor and friends reported finding ten bullet wounds. Sam's pistol was an ordinary six- shooter and Joe's was an automatic, which held a total of seven bullets. If they inflicted all ten or more wounds in Bartell at the time of the killing, then they would have almost emptied their pistols without missing a single shot. If, as is likely, they had missed several times, they might have had to reload their weapons—an even more damning thought. Carriere reported finding only one empty cartridge at the scene of the shooting, but Hut Taylor reported finding an additional six. What of Hut Taylor's credibility? He testified that he had observed blood oozing from Bartell's body on the morning of September 14. That seems dubious in view of the Dr. Westlake's expert testimony to the effect that the body would not still be bleeding that long after death. The evidence concerning the flexibility of the body was also contradictory.

And then there is the bullet hole in Bartell's right shoe. The jurors must have been proud of themselves. They had discerned a pertinent piece of evidence (the interior of the shoe), which the prosecution had apparently overlooked. As we shall see, this evidence, and the manner in which it was brought to the attention of the court, was important for more than one reason. After their seeing the traces of blood in the cut-open shoe, it must have seemed clear to the jury that Bartell had received the bullet wound in his right foot before, or immediately after, the moment of his death. Carriere and the others on the coroner's jury had clearly missed this wound. Had they also missed most of the other wounds, which Hut Taylor and friends claimed to have found on Bartell's body? If so, was their omission intentional or merely negligent? Although there may have been other, less plausible, explanations, the bullet hole in the sole of Bartell's shoe strongly indicated that the Hunts had continued to fire their pistols at Bartell as or after he fell from his horse. Then there was the spent bullet found by Cora Bartell and her uncle at the scene of the shooting six months later. The evidence of this bullet also supported the prosecution's theory that the Hunts had continued to fire at Bartell after he had fallen to the ground.

The jury considered these questions and other matters in evidence until 5:00 PM on Sunday at which time they reported themselves to be deadlocked. They had taken a number of votes, and on all the ballots they had the same split results, nine to three. The judge gave the jurors further instructions and strongly urged that they strive to reach a unanimous verdict. Prior to their being read, the defense strenuously objected to the supplementary jury instructions, but was overruled. The jury again retired, and shortly before noon on Monday, April 8, 1918, they reported having reached a verdict. They found both Sam and Joe Hunt guilty of second-degree murder with a recommendation for clemency.

The Hunts were reported to have reacted stoically to the verdicts, but they must have been stunned and outraged. They were convinced that Bartell had been shooting at them, and they shot back. Where was the crime in that? Unfortunately for the Hunts, the old "Code of the West" had now passed into history, and it had been replaced by criminal codes in which justifiable homicide was much more narrowly defined.

Upon hearing the verdict, the defense gave notice of its intention to submit a motion for a new trial. If this motion were denied, the defense stated that it would then move for an appeal to the New Mexico Supreme Court. Sam and Joe Hunt were ordered by the court to be confined in the Grant County jail pending sentencing. In so far as we know, this was the only time that Sam and Joe were actually in jail in connection with the killing of Chester Bartell.

## The Sentencing

In 1918 there were three noteworthy murder trials in the spring term of the Sixth District Court in Silver City, New Mexico. There were two defendants in each of the three trials, and all six defendants were found guilty of second-degree murder. All six were sentenced by Judge Raymond R. Ryan on Saturday, April 13, 1918. Sam and Joe Hunt received sentences of 40 to 50 years in the New Mexico state penitentiary. The other four defendants each received sentences of 90 to 99 years. The Hunts were reported to have received lower sentences because of their jury's clemency recommendation. As a practical matter, the difference between a 40 to 50 year sentence and a 90 to 99 year sentence is essentially nil. So it would appear that Judge Ryan largely ignored the jury's recommendation for clemency.

Upon receiving the sentence, the defense team for the Hunts entered a motion for a mistrial. We found the full text of the motion in the court records. In the motion the defense asserted a number of grounds for a mistrial. These included:

- The introduction of Bartell's shoes and clothing as evidence, while Cora Bartell was on the stand, was improper. The defense had objected to the introduction of this evidence, contending that the clothing and shoes were irrelevant. The prosecution had then countered that the clothing would provide evidence as to the number and location of bullet wounds to Bartell's body. In its objection, the defense had also raised questions as to whether these items of clothing were actually those worn by Bartell at the time of his death.

- Introduction into evidence of the bullet found by Cora Bartell and her uncle on March 15, 1918 was improper. The contention of the defense was that the bullet's discovery was too remote in time from the killing, and that placing the bullet in evidence during rebuttal was also improper.
- The prosecution should not have been allowed to offer the evidence of the shoe interior after both sides had rested. As with the bullet, this evidence should have been introduced before the prosecution rested its case "in chief."
- The prosecution had failed to show that the killing was unlawful, or that there had been malice aforethought on the part of the defendants.
- When first asking that Bartell's right shoe be cut open, the juror had a communication with the judge outside the hearing of the defense, and such communication was contrary to law.
- The supplementary jury instructions were coercive and otherwise flawed.
- The verdict with a recommendation for clemency was not covered by the jury instructions.
- The verdict was contrary to the evidence.

Essentially all of these issues had been raised by the defense in objections made during the trial, and all such objections had been overruled by the court. It was not surprising then that the motion for granting a new trial was rejected by Judge Ryan. The defense team must have known that the motion for a mistrial stood little chance of success. Apparently, preparing and entering the motion was necessary to preposition the defense for subsequent maneuvers in the case. Immediately after the judge had ruled against the mistrial motion, the defense entered a motion for appealing the convictions of Sam and Joe Hunt to the New Mexico Supreme Court. The appeal motion was granted, and pending the outcome of the appeal, Sam and

Joe were again freed on a bond of $25,000 each. In freeing the defendants on bail, the judge may have thought there was a good possibility of reversible error, or he may have made some concession to the jury's recommendation for clemency after all.

# The First Appeal

With the completion of the first trial, the appeal process began. Jack Hunt was now free of all charges. His brothers, Sam and Joe, were at liberty on bail, but what were essentially life sentences now hung over their heads. It must have been a very tense time. There is some suggestion in the Hunt family lore that Sam and Joe seriously considered emigrating to Brazil or some other foreign country without an extradition treaty with the United States. In 1918, after the trial in April, the Hunts disposed of their property and livestock in the Animas Valley and returned to Southeastern Arizona.

After several months delay, the appeal was forwarded to the New Mexico Supreme Court in Santa Fe. Included in the appeal documents were the attorney's briefs, the verbatim record of the trial testimony, the indictment, bonds, judgment and sentence and various motions, orders and notices issuing from the trial. At more than 1,100 pages, it was quite a bundle of paper. Some of the items of physical evidence introduced in the trial were also sent along to the Supreme Court.

The Supreme Court heard the arguments on the appeal on March 19, 1920. Arguing for the defense were the previously mentioned Clifton Mathews and James S. Casey, and a new member of the defense team, Edward R. Wright of Santa Fe. The prosecution's arguments were presented by the Attorney General for New Mexico, O. O. Asken, and Assistant Attorney General, N. D. Meyer. The syllabus (explanatory summary) and the opinion of the Supreme Court are documented in New Mexico Reports, Volume 26, Pages 160–170. A transcription of the appeal record published in Volume 26 is included herewith as Appendix A.

In their opening brief, the attorneys for the appellants (the defendants) cited three points, which they asserted to constitute reversible errors by the trial court. The appellants descriptions of these three points are taken from their brief and quoted below:

1) *It was error for the trial Court to permit the witness Cora Bartell and the witness Davis McDonald to testify, in rebuttal, over appellants' objections, to the finding of a bullet at the scene of the homicide, more than six months after the date thereof, and to permit the bullet itself to be introduced in evidence.*
2) *After the jury had deliberated for approximately eighteen hours without arriving at a verdict, and had then been called into Court and interrogated by the judge, and, in response to his inquiries, had informed him that they stood then as they had stood since their first ballot, namely, nine to three, without, however, disclosing whether for conviction or acquittal, it was error for the judge to give the jury an additional instruction, inviting them to consider matters other than the law and the evidence, such as the length of time consumed and the expense and trouble occasioned by the trial, telling them repeatedly that it was their duty to agree, warning them against pride of opinion, denouncing as unfaithful to his oath any juror who, in forming or adhering to an opinion, might be influnced [sic] by personal considerations of friendship or business, and urging any juror who might find himself in the minority to seriously question the correctness of his own opinion, simply because of its being a minority opinion, the effect of the whole*

*instruction being to suggest that the minority ought to yield to the majority.*

3) *It was error for the judge to have a conversation with a member of the jury about the case during a recess of the Court, and in the absence and without the knowledge of appellants or their counsel, but in the presence or with the knowledge of the district attorney, and in that conversation to advise the juror to rise in the jury box in open Court, after all evidence and argument had been concluded, and request that the right shoe of the deceased be cut open and exhibited to the jury, and for him afterwards to grant such request when actually made in open Court, never having disclosed to appellants or their counsel that such conversation had been had or such advise given.*

## Point 1

In the argument presented in their brief, the appellants contended that the trial court committed two errors in allowing the introduction of the bullet found by Cora Bartell and her uncle. The appeal brief listed sixteen precedents or authorities (previous appellate court decisions) in support of their arguments against the bullet evidence. First, the defense contended that the bullet was not proper rebuttal evidence, and it should not have been introduced after the prosecution had closed its case "in chief". The Supreme Court found that, even if the facts and circumstances of the bullet evidence were not strictly in rebuttal, the time and manner of the bullet's introduction was within the trial judge's discretion.

Secondly, the bullet had been found at the scene of the killing on March 25, 1918, some six months after the fact. Accordingly, the defense asserted that the finding of the bullet was too remote in time for it to be regarded as valid evidence. The Supreme Court rejected this argument, stating in their opinion, "This second ground is urged for the first time, and, under the well-established rule, is not available to the appellants." It appears that the Supreme Court was off-base on this point. The bullet had been introduced into evidence during the testimony of Davis McDonald. The defense had clearly objected at the time the bullet was offered in evidence, stating, " ... that the finding ... is therefore too remote in point of time." Somehow, the Supreme Court (or its staff) must have missed this part of the transcript. Right or wrong, this Supreme Court ruling on the matter of the bullet evidence would prove to be inconsequential.

As we shall see, the "well-established rule" referred to in the quote above was important in another part of the Supreme Court's decision in the State of New Mexico v. Hunt et al. Appellate courts do not retry cases brought to them on appeal. To win an appeal, an appellant must convince the appellate court that the trial court committed reversible error. Furthermore, the appellant must have made a specific and timely objection to any alleged error during the trial, and thereafter excepted to the judge's adverse ruling on the objection. In other words, if a reversible error were made, the trial judge must have had the opportunity to correct it in the course of the trial. Otherwise, an appellate court will not normally consider untimely assertions of trial court error.

## Point 2

The appellants (the Hunts) sought reversal of the trial court verdict on the ground that the supplemental instructions to the jury had been coercive. Ten precedents were cited. The Supreme Court did take a hard look at the supplementary jury instructions, and they didn't like what they saw. The supplementary instructions called the jurors' attention to the problems, which would ensue from their failure to agree upon a verdict. The instructions further stated that it was the jurors' duty to come to an agreement, if at all possible, and that, among other things, the jurors should not let "personal considerations" affect their deliberations. It was this particular language, which the Supreme Court found objectionable. In its published opinion the Supreme court stated, "It is very doubtful whether the [trial] court was warranted under the law in the use of language which called attention to a possible personal interest of some of the jurors in the case, or a fear of the result upon their personal interests….It was unfortunate language, to say the least"

Despite an apparent inclination to do so, the court did not find the objectionable jury instructions to constitute reversible error. The well-established rule, discussed above, again came into play. The appellants had objected to the supplementary jury instructions before they were read to the jury, but they had complained only of the instructions general coerciveness. At the time of the trial, the defense did not specifically object to the mention of personal considerations in the instructions. Noting this lack of specificity, the Supreme Court ruled, "…this ground of objection was not urged to the instruction of the court below and is not available to the appellants here."

It is noteworthy that, despite its ruling against the appellants on this point, the Supreme Court went to some pains to express and publish its displeasure with the supplementary jury instructions. The justices on the Supreme Court must have wanted to use this opportunity to inform the New Mexico legal community of their position on certain jury instructions.

## Point 3

The last—and pivotal—issue considered by the Supreme Court was the matter of the previously described conversation, between the judge and a juror, in the absence and without the knowledge of the defendants or their counsel. In their brief, the appellants cited 51 precedents in support of their position. In its countering brief, the appellee (the State of New Mexico) cited 10 precedents.

As the appellee (the State) pointed out, this questionable exchange between the juror and the judge was brief and, in the appellee's opinion, innocuous. In addition, it was substantially repeated later in open court and in the presence of the defense. It would not seem unreasonable for the Supreme Court to have found the conversation to have been inconsequential, even though technically wrong. Not so! The Supreme Court came down hard on this point. They held (rather long-windedly) that *any* communication during trial between the judge and jury and outside the hearing of the defense was reversible error. The stricture against such communications may explain the longstanding practice, during trial, of the judge being the last to enter the courtroom and the first to leave. To support its finding on this point, the Supreme Court cited most of the precedents from the appellants' brief and added a few precedents of its own, some dating back as much as a century.

It appears that the Attorney General was very disappointed at the Supreme Court's reversal of the Hunt Brothers' conviction. Accordingly, he petitioned the Supreme Court for a rehearing of the appeal, stating that otherwise, "...a particularly flagitious homicide goes [unpunished], temporarily at least." My dictionary defines flagitious as: shamefully wicked; vile and scandalous. To have resorted to such baroque language, the Attorney General must have really been upset. Pursuant to the petition for rehearing, both sides prepared and submitted additional briefs. The Supreme Court considered and then denied the petition for a rehearing, and its decision on the appeal stood.

Having found reversible error as described above, the Supreme Court of New Mexico issued an order, dated June 30, 1920, reversing the second-degree murder convictions of Sam and Joe Hunt, and remanding the case to the 6th District Court for retrial.

Sam and Joe had received another reprieve, but the murder charges still hung over them.

# The Second Trial

Sometime in 1918, the New Mexico legislature split off the southern end of Grant County to form Hidalgo County. Lordsburg was designated as the county seat for Hidalgo County, and a new courthouse was constructed there. Hidalgo County and its court remained a part of 6th Judicial District. Because the killing of Chester Bartell had occurred in what was now Hidalgo County, the second murder trial of Sam and Joe Hunt took place in Lordsburg.

The retrial of State of New Mexico vs. Samuel L. Hunt and Joseph S. Hunt was assigned Case (or Cause) No. 11. The trial of Case No. 11 began on Monday, May 23, 1921. This time Sam and Joe Hunt were charged with second-degree murder in the death of Chester Bartell. Their previous convictions of second-degree murder (Case No. 7015) precluded their being again charged with first-degree murder. Jack Hunt, having been found not guilty in the earlier case, was not charged in Case No. 11.

The State of New Mexico was represented in Case No. 11 by District Attorney Forrest Fiedler and by J. S. Vaught, the former district attorney. Vaught had been the lead prosecutor in the first trial in Silver City. The defense team was again led by Clifton Mathews. He was assisted by Percy Wilson and W. B. Walton, both of Silver City. Apparently, the case was initially assigned to Judge Raymond

R. Ryan, and he signed some of the preliminary orders for Case No. 11. Judge Ryan had presided over the first trial in Silver City, and he properly recused himself from hearing evidence in the second trial in Lordsburg. He was replaced by Judge Edwin Mechem of the third Judicial District. Judge Mechem's brother, Merritt C. Mechem, was the then current governor of New Mexico. Incidentally, Mr. Walton, of the defense team, was a former US congressman. Percy Wilson, also a member of the defense team, was the current and longtime mayor of Silver City. There is no indication that the presence of these political luminaries had much impact on the trial. They must have, however, attracted some attention to the proceedings.

An article in the May 26, 1921 issue the *Lordsburg Liberal* provided some details about the trial in Lordsburg and related events. That article was not, however, as comprehensive as the one published after the first trial on April 19, 1918 in the *Silver City Independent*. The *Liberal* article is a typical, and somewhat amusing, example of small town journalism at the time. A transcription of the *Liberal* article is included herewith as Appendix C.

The first day of the trial was consumed by the jury selection. The jurors were selected from an existing pool of jurors, and its selection took much less time than in the previous trial. Again a jury of twelve, apparently all anglo, men were chosen.

## The Testimony

On Tuesday, the prosecution began presenting its case. With some exceptions, the prosecution case was presented in much the same way as before. Cora Bartell's testimony was essentially the same as in the first trial. She did note that Sam Hunt's homestead, the Eldridge Place, had since been acquired by her sister's husband, Henry Eicks. Cora Bartell's testimony again included reference to the visit she and her uncle had made to the scene of Chester Bartell's death some six months afterward. She mentioned the bullet that they had then found at the scene. As before, the defense objected to the bullet's admission in evidence, again asserting that the finding of the bullet was too remote in time. This time the court sustained the objection, and nothing further was said about the bullet.

Amos Taylor was the next prosecution witness. His father, W. H. (Hut) Taylor, was now dead, and in his stead, Amos described the ten bullet wounds in Bartell's body that he, his father and others had reportedly found on the morning after the shooting. Amos Taylor did not, nor could he, give testimony about the discoveries made by his father and Tobe Lacey when they visited the scene of the shooting on September 15, 1917. Otherwise, Amos' testimony seemed to confirm the significant statements by his father in the first trial. Amos Taylor identified the clothing that Bartell had been wearing at the time of his death, including the infamous, now cut-open, right shoe with its bullet hole and remnants of blood. The clothing items were admitted in evidence, and Amos pointed out several presumed bullet holes and bloodstains in the clothing. Amos also noted that Cora Bartell was his first cousin. Tobe Lacey did not testify in this second trial.

Following Amos Taylor to the witness stand, were Fred Sanford, Joe Yarbrough, W. P. Birchfield and James Morehead. These four were all part of the group called in by Hut Taylor to witness the reexamination of Bartell's body at Taylor's ranch on the morning of September 14, 1917. All four substantially corroborated the testimony of Amos Taylor concerning the bullet wounds found in Bartell's body.

William H. McDonald, one of Cora Bartell's uncles, was the next prosecution witness. He told of his bringing a casket to Hut Taylor's place on September 15, 1917 and subsequently using the casket to transport Bartell's body to Arizona for burial. McDonald corroborated the testimony of previous prosecution witnesses as to the number and location of bullet holes in Bartell's body. When picking up the body, McDonald was accompanied by Henry Eicks, Cora Bartell's brother-in-law. McDonald also noted that at the time of the second trial (May 1921) Henry Eicks owned the Eldridge Place, the homestead which Sam Hunt had previously filed on.

Jack Hunt was again called as a prosecution witness. As before, he recounted the sequence of events on the morning of September 13, 1917, which led up to the encounter between his brothers and Chester Bartell. His testimony concluded with a description of the shooting scene. Chester Bartell was lying on the ground, apparently dead, and Sam and Joe were sitting nearby on their horses, still holding their pistols. The defense attorney did not cross-examine Jack, stating that Jack would be later called as a defense witness. Jack was excused, and at this point, the prosecution rested its case. It was now midday on Tuesday, and the court recessed for lunch.

On Tuesday afternoon, the defense opened its case by moving for a directed verdict of acquittal, asserting that the prosecution had failed to prove the charges. The motion was denied, and the defense began presenting evidence. As with the prosecution, the defense case was similar to that in the first trial, except, as we shall see, there would be significant testimony from three new defense witnesses.

Jack Hunt was again called to the witness stand, this time as the first defense witness. As when testifying in the previous trial, Jack told of his being born and raised in Texas, his coming to Arizona, his working there and his eventually coming to the Animas Valley in June 1917. Jack's brothers, Sam and Joe, relocated to the Animas Valley before him, arriving there in the fall of 1916. Jack noted that he was then (May 1921) 39 years old and was now married. Sam and Joe were both still single and were then 35 and 25, respectively.

Jack left the Eldridge Place in the Animas Valley around the first of the year, 1918 and relocated with his parents to his cousin's ranch in nearby Guadalupe Canyon. (Jack's cousin, Stewart Hunt, owned and lived on the ranch in Guadalupe Canyon. Jack and his brothers had worked closely with Stewart for many years.) The Guadalupe Canyon ranch was also in New Mexico. It was about twelve miles southwest of the Eldridge Place, and closer to the Arizona border. In April 1920, Jack moved back to Cochise County, Arizona, and at the time of the trial, he was still living in Cochise County, near Douglas.

Jack again told of he, Sam and Joe driving a small herd of cattle along the trail from the Eldridge Place to the Blair Place on the morning of September 13, 1917. Their intention was to take the cattle to a watering place near the trail and about a mile and three quarters from the Eldridge Place. The trail was located entirely on either their own land or their US Forest leasehold. Again Jack told of his leaving the trail to turn back some straying cattle, and while so engaged hearing a number of gunshots. He then joined his brothers at the scene of the shooting and observed Bartell's presumably dead body lying on the ground. Jack, Sam and Joe then left the scene. Sam and Joe headed east toward the open part of the Animas Valley, and Jack rode southeast about one and a half miles back to the Hunt ranch house, arriving about 11:30 AM.

Jack told of seeing two men on horseback ominously lurking in some brush near the house, and of eventually going inside for lunch. Cora Bartell then made her appearance and asked Jack to go with her to where Bartell's body was lying on the ground. Jack demurred, didn't tell Cora about the shooting, and proceeded by car to find the authorities. Jack found Carriere, the justice of the peace, and returned home with him, having encountered Sam and Joe along the way. That evening Jack accompanied Carriere and the coroner's jury to the scene of the shooting, and observed their examination of Bartell's body. Jack then took Carriere in his car down the valley some twenty miles where they found Charles Johnson, the deputy sheriff. Jack, Carriere and Johnson then returned to the Hunt ranch. Along the way they stopped at the home of Hut Taylor, and Carriere received Taylor's permission to deliver Bartell's body to Taylor's home. Meanwhile arrangements had been made to transport the body in one of the Hunts' wagons.

Jack was again vigorously cross-examined by the prosecution, but nothing came out that conflicted significantly with his previous testimony. On redirect and over the objections of the prosecution, Jack was able to explain that he and his brothers were armed on September 13, 1917 because of threatening gunfire which had, shortly before, been directed at or near them. Jack told of he and deputy sheriff Johnson going to Bisbee together on September 15, 1917. No explanation for this visit was given.

Sam Hunt was the next defense witness. His testimony in the second (Lordsburg) trial did not vary significantly from that in the first trial. He was now 35 years old. When asked if he were married, he said yes. I believe this is in error. Either Sam didn't understand the question or the court recorder erred in recording his answer. Nothing in record or memory of anyone in the family indicates that Sam ever married. At the time of the second trial, Sam was living in Warren, a suburb of Bisbee, Arizona, and was again working in the Bisbee mines. Sam ruefully noted that he had relinquished his claim to the Eldridge Place in August 1919, only two or three weeks before he would have "proved up." I believe this means that had Sam been able to prove up, he would have received a patent or deed to the Eldridge Place homestead. Sam also indicated his resentment at the Eldridge Place having subsequently fallen into the possession of Henry Eicks, Cora Bartell's brother-in-law. Sam's felony murder conviction in April 1918 may have made him ineligible for a patent under the Homestead Act.

As in the first trial, Sam was closely examined and cross-examined about his activities on September 13, 1917. His testimony was essentially the same as before. The photographs of the shooting scene that had been introduced in the first trial were again introduced while Sam was on the witness stand. Sam again used the photographs in describing the events just prior to and during the shooting. He again stated emphatically that he had fired his pistol at Bartell only five times and that he did not fire at Bartell after he had fallen from his horse.

Joe Hunt was the next to testify. At the time of the second trial (May 1921), Joe was 25 years old and still single. He had left the Animas Valley in the spring of 1918 and moved to Bisbee. He then worked in the mines in Bisbee until shortly before the second trial began. Joe told of his volunteering for service in the US Army in August of 1917, but then never having been called up for such service.

As with his brothers, Joe's testimony in the second trial was essentially the same as in the first trial. He again told of the incidents on September 7, 8, 9 and 10, 1917, when he believed that Bartell had fired a rifle at or near him. He also again stated that, on September 13, 1917, he had only fired three rounds at Bartell and had quit firing when Bartell fell from his horse.

Next came the three new defense witnesses. They were new in that they did not testify in the first trial. Their names were Mount Manning, William Swyer and Don A. Sullivan. Manning was the first of these three to take the stand.

Manning was a range inspector for the Arizona Livestock Sanitary Board. His primary duty was investigating reports of cattle rustling in Arizona. In carrying out his duties, he was empowered by the State of Arizona to pursue and arrest suspected cow thieves. In early March 1917 he had a conversation with Chester Bartell on a street in Douglas. He stated that Bartell approached him and asserted that Sam and Joe Hunt were stealing cattle over in New Mexico.

Manning was apparently acquainted with the Hunt family and told Bartell he was mistaken about the Hunts being cattle thieves. Bartell insisted that the Hunts were stealing cattle, and that he wanted the Hunts arrested and sent to prison for cattle rustling. He asked Manning to cooperate with him in a scheme for trapping and incriminating the Hunts. Bartell proposed to gather some calves belonging to another rancher in New Mexico. Bartell would put the Hunts' brand on the calves, and then herd the calves across the border into Arizona and into Manning's possession. According to the scheme, Manning would then arrest the Hunts, citing the misbranded calves as evidence. Sam and Joe Hunt could then be convicted of cattle rustling and sent to prison. Manning emphatically refused to participate in any such scheme. Bartell then told Manning that, "there's $5,000 in it for us, if we get them boys [the Hunts] out." Manning still refused to help Bartell with his scheme, after which Bartell said, "Well, I am going to get them [the Hunts] out of the country if I have to kill them myself."

Manning was aggressively cross-examined by the prosecution. Manning stuck by his story, but he did admit that Dr. Charles Hunt (the older brother of Sam and Joe) had paid some of his travel expenses in coming to Lordsburg to testify at the trial. Manning also explained why he had not testified in the first trial. He heard about the shooting of Bartell sometime in the fall of 1917. Shortly thereafter, the Arizona Sanitary Board transferred Manning to a remote area in Northern Arizona. While in Northern Arizona, he did not have access to newspapers or other sources of news, and Manning did not learn of the Hunts being charged with murder until after they had been convicted in April 1918.

William Swyer was the next to testify. He stated that he had been with Manning, when Bartell approached him in Douglas in early March 1917. He also said that he heard essentially all of the conversation between Bartell and Manning, and confirmed Manning's version of the conversation. Swyer joined the US Navy in December 1917 and spent most of the next three years at sea. He, too, did not learn that Sam and Joe Hunt were charged with murder until after they had been convicted in the first trial.

The last of the three new witnesses to take the stand was Don A. Sullivan. In 1917, Sullivan was a forest ranger stationed at Skeleton Canyon in the Peloncillo Mountains. Sullivan's area of responsibility as a forest ranger included the Blair Place and the other US Forest lands, which the Hunts had under lease. The head of Skeleton Canyon is in New Mexico and about five miles north of the Blair Place. From there, the canyon drains northwest into Arizona. Incidentally, the renegade Apache leader, Geronimo, was captured in Skeleton Canyon near the Arizona-New Mexico border.

Around September 1, 1917, Chester Bartell approached Sullivan and asked that he be given a lease or permit for the forest service land that Hunts already had under lease. Sullivan told Bartell that he could not give him a permit for that parcel for several reasons, the primary reason being that the Hunts had a valid, paid-up lease. There were other qualifications that Bartell would have to meet before he could receive a lease on any forest parcel. Bartell asserted to Sullivan that his family had previously owned land adjoining the Hunt lease, and he thereby had a prior right to the lease. According to Sullivan, Bartell also said, "All you got to do is give me a permit. I will clear that range so far as the Hunts are concerned." Sullivan refused to even accept an application for a forest lease from Bartell. He advised Bartell that he might be able to obtain a forest permit, when and if additional forest parcels were opened for lease the following year.

Sullivan stated that some time prior to the first trial (April 1918), he had been transferred by the forest service to oversee an area located above the Mogollon Rim in Arizona. In that remote location, he had very limited access to a post office or other sources of information. Accordingly, he, like the two foregoing witnesses, did not learn of the first trial until after it was concluded.

The defense next called seven character witnesses: Captain Harry C. Wheeler, Charles E. Cross, Captain M. E. Cassidy, "Professor" Harry Crocket, Fred Sanford, William P. Birchfield, Jr. and Holmes Maddox. All of these witnesses stated unequivocally that Sam and Joe Hunt both had good reputations and were quiet, peaceable, and law-abiding men.

Of the character witnesses, Wheeler was the best known. As the Sheriff of Cochise County, Arizona, he had organized and overseen the famous (or infamous) Bisbee Deportation in the summer of 1917. In the "deportation," Wheeler and his allies gathered up members and supporters of the International Workers of the World (IWW) at gunpoint. The IWW was a militant, leftist labor union, which had infuriated the copper industry establishment in Bisbee. After they had been rounded up, the adherents of the IWW or "Wobblies" were forcibly loaded on a train, which transported them out of Bisbee and then deposited them at a remote desert location in New Mexico. Roadblocks were afterward set up to prevent the Wobblies from returning to Bisbee. Wheeler was a colorful character, who was much admired by his supporters and detested with equal passion by his detractors. Albert Nowlin, a brother-in-law of the Hunt brothers, was an active participant with Wheeler in herding the Wobblies out of Bisbee.

Cross was a deputy sheriff in Cochise County and had been a policeman in Douglas. Cassidy was a retired army officer of some distinction and at the time of the trial was an executive with the Phelps Dodge Corporation in Bisbee. Harry Crocket was a public school teacher in Bisbee and a boyhood friend of Joe Hunt. Sanford,

Birchfield and Maddox were cattle ranchers in the Animas Valley. Sanford and Birchfield had also been witnesses for the prosecution. Maddox was the last of the defense witnesses.

Amos Taylor was next recalled as a rebuttal witness by the prosecution. He testified that he had passed by the scene of Bartell's shooting on a number of occasions and asserted that the trail did not fork there as the Hunts had contended in their testimony.

The prosecution then put Davis McDonald, another of Cora Bartell's uncles, on the stand as a rebuttal witness. He also said that he was familiar with the trail between the Eldridge and Blair Places and that the trail did not fork at or near the scene of the shooting. McDonald also stated that, prior to the Hunts arrival, the Eldridge Place had been owned by Lee Ramsey and before that by Chap Howard. He also noted that Lee Ramsey and Chap Howard were both relatives of his. He further stated that Henry Eicks had succeeded Sam Hunt as owner of the Eldridge Place, and at the time of trial, Eicks was still the owner. Eicks was married to McDonald's niece.

Cora Bartell testified again, this time in rebuttal. Mrs. Bartell stated that she had been with or near her husband and continuously knew of his whereabouts on September 7, 8, 9 and 10, 1917. This testimony conflicted with Joe Hunt's assertions that Bartell had shot at him several times during that period.

Cora also stated that, in early March 1917, she and her husband were contemplating settling on a homestead in Arizona, near Douglas. She said that they did not decide to settle instead in the Animas Valley until the end of May 1917. This testimony was apparently intended to counter the testimony of Mount Manning and William Swyer. Those two had told of Manning's conversation with Chester Bartell in March 1917, in which conversation Bartell had indicated his desire to drive the Hunts out of the Animas Valley and had even mentioned killing the Hunts.

Cora Bartell also corroborated the assertions by Amos Taylor and Davis McDonald that there was not a fork in the trail at or near the scene of Bartell's shooting. For reasons that are not entirely clear, the prosecution really stressed this point. The Hunts had all testified that the trail had so forked. In trying to refute this, the prosecution may have been hoping to call other aspects of the Hunts' testimony into question. Cora Bartell was the last witness to testify at the second trial in Lordsburg. She left the witness stand late in the evening on Wednesday.

## Conclusion Of The Trial

Thursday began with a closing argument from District Attorney Fielder. He was followed by an impassioned summary of the defense version of the case by Clifton Mathews. The defense position was further supported by an eloquent presentation by W. H. Walton, the former congressman. The closing arguments concluded with what was described as a presentation of extraordinary merit by the prosecutor, J. S. Vaught. Judge Mechem then read his lengthy instructions to the jury, and apparently late in the day on Thursday, the jury retired to consider the case. Again, a copy of the jury instructions was found in the Supreme Court records.

With several significant exceptions, essentially all of the evidence presented in the second trial had been introduced in the first trial. The most important of these exceptions was the testimony from the three new defense witnesses, Manning, Swyer and Sullivan. Their testimony clearly contradicted Cora Bartell's contention that her husband had only innocent intentions, when he started out to visit the Hunts on the morning of September 13, 1917. If the jurors in the first trial had been better informed of Bartell's malevolent intentions toward the Hunts, they might well have come to a different verdict.

In this connection, it is noteworthy that, in the early ballots, three of the jurors in the first trial had apparently voted for acquittal.

Surprisingly, some of what seemed to have been crucial testimony for the defense in the first trial was missing from the second. The Justice of the Peace, Carriere, did not testify, nor were any of the other members of the coroner's jury heard from. Carriere and the other members of the coroner's jury asserted in the first trial that there were only two bullet wounds in Bartell's body. Their absence from the second trial left uncontested the Taylors' claim of finding of up to ten wounds. There was also no testimony by Dr. O. J. Westlake or any other medical professional regarding how and when bullet wounds would bleed.

In addition, Hut Taylor, who had been the prosecution's star witness in the first trial, did not testify in the second trial. This was simply because he had died some time during the period between the two trials. For whatever reason, Tobe Lacey was apparently not available to testify again. And as noted above, the evidence of the bullet found six months after the shooting was not admitted.

There was also a significant difference between the instructions given to the juries in the two trials. In the first trial, Judge Ryan gave the jury three verdict choices, guilty of first-degree murder, guilty of second-degree murder or innocent by reason of self-defense. In the second trial, Judge Mechem told the jury that they could find the defendants guilty of either second-degree murder or manslaughter, or they could be found not guilty by reason of self-defense. Before the instructions were read to the jury, the defense objected to the inclusion of manslaughter in the instructions. The basis of the objection being that the facts of the case could not support a manslaughter finding. The objection was overruled.

As before, the jury was confronted with conflicting interpretations of the evidence in the case. After deliberating through the night, the jury returned to the courtroom and announced their verdict on Friday morning. They reported having been split initially as follows: four for acquittal, four for manslaughter and four for second-degree murder. They finally unanimously agreed to find both defendants guilty of manslaughter. Upon receiving and accepting the jury's verdict, the judge proceeded to give both defendants a sentence of seven to nine years in the state penitentiary. The defense took exceptions to both the judgment and the sentence, and moved for an appeal to the Supreme Court of New Mexico. The court granted the appeal motion and freed both defendants pending appeal on bail of $5,000 each. Remarkably, receiving the verdict, pronouncing the sentence, entering and granting the motion for appeal, and freeing of the defendants on bail all took place on one day, Friday, May 27, 1921.

Sam and Joe Hunt could now breathe a little easier. Seven to nine years in the penitentiary was not a pleasant prospect, but it was a lot better than forty to fifty years. And there was the possibility that the appeal of the second conviction would be successful.

## Miscellany

As previously noted, the article in the *Lordsburg Liberal* did not cover the actual trial testimony in much detail. The editor explained this by stating, "The *Liberal* never cares to go into grewsome [sic] details of an alleged murder." Although its readers were spared the "grewsome" details, the newspaper did provide some trivia about those attending the trial.

Several of these observations were as follows:

- There was "standing room only" in the courtroom during the trial.
- David and W. M. McDonald, uncles of Cora Bartell, attended the trial.

- All five of the Hunt Brothers(Charlie, Jim, Jack, Sam and Joe) were non-tobacco users.
- The trial was attended by a good many ladies and high school students.
- Professor Crockett teaches printing in the Bisbee public schools.
- Mrs. Chester (Cora) Bartell, widow of the deceased, and her small son, Norman were pathetic figures in court.
- Captain M. E. Cassidy and the editor had served together at Camp Cody (presumably an army base).
- In addition to the character witnesses the following family members and friends of the Hunts attended the trial:
  Mr. And Mrs. John B. Rawlings, formerly of Bisbee;
  Charles Cross, former deputy sheriff in Bisbee;
  Mrs. E. B. Rider and Bessie Hunt, sisters of the defendants;
  Miss Alice Crone, a family friend from New York;
  W. A. (Albert) Nowlin, brother-in-law of the defendants;
  Miss Kennedy of Bisbee (This was undoubtedly Edith Kennedy, future wife of Joe Hunt and, eventually, my mother.);
  Earl B. Thompson of Bisbee.

# The Second Appeal

On December 22, 1924, the Supreme Court of New Mexico announced its decision on the appeal of the manslaughter convictions in State of New Mexico vs. Samuel L. and Joseph P. Hunt. The court must have had a crowded docket. The convictions under appeal had been pronounced, over three years before, on May 27, 1921.

On appeal, Sam and Joe Hunt were again represented by the legal defense team of Clifton Mathews, Percy Wilson and W. B. Walton. Arguments for the State were presented by the Attorney General, Milton J. Helmick, and his assistant, John W. Armstrong.

The Supreme Court published its syllabus and opinion for this appeal in New Mexico Reports, Volume 30, Pages 273--276. For a legal document, the opinion by Justice C. J. Parker (or his law clerk) is refreshingly intelligible and succinct. With the minor exception of some of the precedent citations, the Supreme Court's published opinion is quoted below in it its entirety.

## *Opinion Of The Court*

*PARKER, C. J. This case was before this court once before, and was reversed for considerations not pertinent to this inquiry. See State v. Hunt, 26 N. M.160, 189 P.1111. Over the objection of appellants, the court in this trial submitted to the jury the question of guilt of appellants [Sam and Joe Hunt] of voluntary manslaughter. The trial resulted in a conviction of voluntary manslaughter, and this is the sole question presented for review. The facts in the case are, briefly stated: That on the morning of September 13, 1917, the deceased [Bartell] left his homestead on horseback to go to the Hunt Place, some four or five miles distant, where appellants and their brother, Jack P. Hunt, lived with their parents and sister. When the deceased left his home, he had with him a 30-30 Winchester rifle, which he carried in a scabbard on the right-hand side of his saddle. He was riding along a trail which led through rocks and brushes to the point where his body was afterwards found. His body showed numerous bullet wounds, which were the cause of his death. On the morning of said September 13, 1917, the appellants, together with their brother, Jack P. Hunt, started out to drive some cattle from the Hunt place to what is called the Blair place, for the purpose of taking the cattle to a watering place situated on the Blair place. The Hunts were all armed with rifles and pistols. In so driving the cattle, they drove them along the same trail upon which the deceased was traveling toward them. At the point where they met the deceased, the trail divided, and one branch went around either side of a clump of bushes, through or beyond which the appellants could not see a man on horseback. Just prior to reaching the clump of bushes, some of the cattle which they were driving left the trail, and the brother, Jack. P. Hunt, left the trail to go after and return the cattle, and he was not present at the killing. One of the appellants passed to the right and the other to the left of the clump of bushes, and upon arriving at the farther side of the bushes they saw the deceased sitting on his horse, his horse standing still, the deceased holding the bridle reins in his left hand and attempting with his right hand to take his Winchester out of the scabbard in which he was carrying the same. The gun hung in the scabbard, and the deceased was never able to get the gun more than halfway out of the scabbard. Not a word was spoken by any of the three parties. Upon seeing the deceased drawing his Winchester from the scabbard, the two appellants opened fire upon him with pistols, discharging several shots, and keeping on firing until the deceased began to fall from his horse to the ground, where he instantly died. Jack P. Hunt, upon* *hearing the shots, came to the spot, and the three Hunts left together; Jack Hunt going at once to the justice of the peace and announcing the killing, and the two appellants going to or near the Hunt place, where they surrendered themselves to the justice of the peace. The Hunts account for the fact that they were armed by testifying that one of them had been shot at on three different occasions by some unknown person about a week prior to the homicide, and that they believed that the deceased was the person who fired the shot. Prior to that time, they had gone unarmed. Witnesses testified in behalf of appellants that the deceased tried to employ them to assist him in getting the Hunts out of the country, and said that there was $5,000 in it if it could be done, and that he (the deceased) was going to get them out if he had to kill them himself. Appellants were not informed of this threat until after the homicide. A forest ranger also testified that deceased tried to get him to give deceased a permit covering the same land which the Hunts had already procured from the Forest Service, which he declined to do, and that the deceased told him that he wanted to run the Hunts off of the Blair place, which was the place for which he desired the forest ranger to give him a permit. The evidence seems to be uncontradicted in any material particular. The Attorney General seeks to sustain the instruction of the court by arguing that the evidence justifies the inference that there was, or might have been, heat of passion in the minds of the appellants. He suggests that shooting at one of the appellants by deceased about a week previous to the homicide was adequate cause for heat of passion in the form of fear and terror. He also suggests the presence of the deceased on the trail, causing the cattle to stampede, the watering of deceased's horse at appellants watering place without leave, and the mere fact of the trespass of deceased by being on the trail and on the land covered by the forest permit of the appellants, as possible adequate cause for heat of passion. It is perfectly apparent that none of these facts are adequate cause for heat of passion, and if appellants killed deceased for any one or all of these reasons, they murdered him. The former shooting, if they had reason to believe and did believe that deceased had done it, they might take into consideration in viewing the situation when the deceased made the deadly assault upon them, if he did. If he made no such assault, appellants murdered him. If he did make the assault,* *and appellants, as ordinarily reasonable men, had reason to believe and did believe in the imminence of danger to their lives, or danger of great bodily harm to them, from such assault, they were justified in the killing on the ground of self-defense.*

*This case was tried at a time when the law in this jurisdiction was in some confusion owing to a concurring opinion in State v. Kidd, 24 N. M.... in which it was stated that a defendant could not complain of a conviction of a lower degree of unlawful homicide than was shown by the evidence. Since that time, however, the whole matter has been cleared up, and it is now the settled law that it is error, requiring reversal, to submit a degree of homicide not within the proofs, and over the objection of the defendant. See State v. Pruett ....*

*The appellants have been acquitted of murder, and cannot be shown to be guilty of manslaughter. They are therefore entitled to be discharged.*

*It follows that the judgment is erroneous and should be reversed, and the cause remanded, with directions to discharge the appellants; and it is so ordered.*

*BOTTS and FORT, JJ. concur.*

In the trial in Lordsburg, Judge Mechem had to exclude first-degree murder from consideration, but as previously noted, he gave the jurors the option of finding Sam and Joe Hunt guilty of second-degree murder, guilty of manslaughter or innocent by reason of self-defense. Judge Mechem's instructions clearly stated that for the defendants to be guilty of manslaughter, the jurors had to find that Sam and Joe Hunt had killed Bartell without "malice," but had to have been acting instead in the "heat of passion."

Legal professionals are inclined to ponder and argue about the fine distinctions between simmering anger and instantaneous passion. Indeed that was the central issue in the Supreme Court Opinion quoted above, but the lay jurors in Lordsburg were probably not into such esoterica. I suggest that the jury's reasoning for its manslaughter verdicts was as follows. Despite Bartell's aggressive acts, Sam and Joe Hunt had wrongfully killed him. Ten bullet wounds could hardly be ignored. On the other hand, Sam and Joe appeared, through their own conduct and the testimony of character witnesses, to be upstanding young fellows. Accordingly, the harsh sentences likely to result from murder convictions seemed inappropriate. The milder sanctions from manslaughter convictions would be sufficient punishment. After their first ballot (four for second-degree murder, four for manslaughter and four for acquittal) the obvious compromise was manslaughter and so it was.

Judge Mechem could have been criticized by the Supreme Court for even allowing the jury to consider a manslaughter verdict. However, in its opinion, the court gave Judge Mechem some cover (Judge Mechem was the governor's brother.) by noting that there had previously been confusion in the New Mexico courts as to whether manslaughter could be treated as a lesser-included offense under second-degree murder. By the time the Supreme Court had reviewed the manslaughter convictions of Sam and Joe Hunt, this matter had been "cleared up," and a manslaughter conviction not "within the proofs" required reversal.

On the evening of December 22, 1924, Joe Hunt's friends in Bisbee threw a party to celebrate the decision announced earlier that day by the New Mexico Supreme Court. The ordeal did not officially end until February 21, 1925. On that date, Judge Raymond R. Ryan (the same Judge Ryan, who had presided over the first trial) of New Mexico's Sixth Judicial District signed an order, which reopened State of New Mexico vs. Samuel L. Hunt and Joseph S. Hunt and, in compliance with the Supreme Court's mandate, discharged the defendants. Free at last.

# The Principal Players

Sam and Joe Hunt may have finally beaten the murder charges, but the killing of Chester Bartell had far-reaching, adverse consequences for them and their family. Joe was only twenty-two years old in 1917, and he had only recently joined his three older brothers in the cattle ranching business. Those three, Jim, Jack and Sam were in the prime of their lives in 1917. They were all healthy, seasoned and capable cattlemen. By 1917 they had, along with their cousin, Stewart Hunt, acquired substantial amounts of land and livestock. The cattle business was thriving, and they were well positioned for greater prosperity. However, the "troubles," which was how they referred to the killing of Bartell and its aftermath, drastically lessened their business prospects.

The spiritual toll was even heavier. The Hunt tribe, which included the four brothers in the cattle business, their parents, their older brother, their five sisters and assorted spouses and children, constituted a tight, nuclear family. Sam and Joe were particularly bright and full of promise. The awful prospect of those two young men being in prison for many years bore down heavily on every member of the family and on a wide group of friends as well. Photo No. 2 on page 15 shows what all five of the Hunt brothers looked like in 1920.

The financial demands rising out of the troubles were enormous. The Hunts were compelled to engage a team of prestigious and expensive lawyers. The services of these lawyers continued off and on for the entire seven years of the ordeal. The bail bonds had to have been another large financial burden. At one point in time, Jack, Sam and Joe were all three charged with first-degree murder, and each was under a $25,000 bond. The combined bail amount totaling $75,000 would be the modern day equivalent of about $1,000,000. Even if they only had to actually post a fraction of the bond, it still would have been a substantial sum. The family pooled and sold off its assets to cover these financial burdens. They apparently also had some financial assistance from several wealthy benefactors from in and around Bisbee. Their Animas Valley ranch land and its livestock had to be sold, very likely at distressed prices, and the Hunts resettled back in Southeastern Arizona.

## JOSEPH STUART HUNT

Around 1902 at the age of seven, Joe Hunt came to Arizona from his birthplace near Comfort, Texas. He was the baby of his family, being the last of ten children. However, since he was largely raised by his older sister, Caroline, he was virtually her oldest child. The Hunts were a close knit family, so while growing up, Joe also lived at various times with his parents and with his other siblings. He attended public schools in both Bisbee and Douglas. His formal education ended with his graduation from Douglas High School in 1914. Joe Hunt was nearly six feet tall, strongly built, athletic and handsome (See Photo No. 3 on page 85). He was also personable, well-liked and, unlike most of his siblings, a gregarious extrovert. As he grew up, Joe became a popular young man about town in both Bisbee and Douglas.

*Arizona State Senator Joe S. Hunt, circa 1935, official photograph from Arizona State Archives.*

After leaving the Animas Valley and while the murder charges were pending, Joe Hunt returned to Bisbee and worked for a time in the copper mines there. In 1924 he became the director of boys activities at the Bisbee YMCA, and he served in that capacity with some distinction for four years. At about the time of his marriage to Edith Kennedy in 1928, he moved to the John Slaughter Ranch, which is located about fifteen miles east of Douglas. The Slaughter Ranch, also known as the San Bernardino Ranch, had been leased by the Hunts, and Joe was now a full partner with his brothers in their cattle ranching operations. Ironically, the Slaughter Ranch is only about 25 miles west of the Animas Valley.

While at the Slaughter Ranch, Joe became actively involved in politics. In 1934 and again in 1936 he successfully ran for the Arizona State Senate, representing Cochise County. During this same period, Joe also became an active member of the Arizona Cattle Growers Association, and eventually he was elected to the vice presidency of the statewide organization. Joe and Edith Hunt had two sons. My brother (Joseph Phillip) was born in 1930, and I (Norman Kennedy) was born in 1934. In 1937 the Hunt partnership was dissolved, and Joe and his brother, Jack, jointly purchased and moved to the Honeymoon Ranch, north of Clifton, Arizona. On October 6, 1940, the life and promising career of Joe Hunt ended. He was thrown from a horse and fatally injured. Joe was 45 years old. At the time of his death, a campaign committee had been formed and was actively making plans to run Joe S. Hunt for the office of Arizona Governor.

## SAMUEL LEROY HUNT

Sam was born in Texas in 1885. Of the ten children in the family, only Sam and his oldest brother, Charlie, attended college. Sam studied engineering, but never really practiced that profession. Shortly after leaving college around 1908, Sam joined his brothers and cousins in their various business enterprises, primarily cattle ranching. After the "troubles" began in New Mexico, Sam moved back to Bisbee.

Sam was a good-looking man, but a little shorter and stockier than his younger brother Joe. Sam was apparently rather shy, and never married. Around 1920 he and his unmarried sister, Bess, moved to Southern California. Two of his married sisters and their families also ended up living in or near Los Angeles. Sam leased a small ranch in the hills east of La Habra, California, where he and Bess lived until he retired in the late 1950s. Sam ran a few cattle on the ranch, but worked full time as a cattle inspector in the Los Angeles stockyards. He eventually rose to be the chief inspector, supervising a staff of about twelve. Sam retired in La Habra and died there in the early sixties.

## JOHN PARTRIDGE HUNT

Jack Hunt was born in Titus County, Texas in 1881. At the age of 18 he left the family home near Comfort, Texas and followed his older brother, Jim, and their cousin, Stewart, to Arizona. He arrived in Bisbee in 1900 (He called it nineteen ought, ought.). He worked for a time in the copper mines in Bisbee, but soon joined his brother and cousin in their horse and cattle ranching ventures. They ran the Rancho Sacatal west of Douglas for about ten years. They also had cattle operations in Mexico, did some farming around Yuma, Arizona and for a time owned and operated a slaughter house in Douglas.

When Jack and his parents left the Animas Valley in the summer of 1918, they did not return directly to Arizona. Instead, they spent some time on the ranch in Guadalupe Canyon, which belonged to Jack's cousin, Stewart Hunt. While there, Jack met and eventually married Sally Stewart. Jack and Sally were not themselves related, but both were first cousins of Stewart Hunt.

While Jack and family were in Guadalupe Canyon, there was again more trouble with their hostile neighbors. Shots were fired at the Guadalupe Canyon ranch house from the ridges above the house. On one occasion, Jack's father was shaving, when a bullet crashed through the window next to him. Jack resolved to put an end to this harassment.

He armed himself and set out in search of the assailants. He told the family that his intention was to find and kill them. If he were successful in this effort, he would not return home. Instead, he would tie his handkerchief to the gatepost below the house and go down the Guadalupe Canyon and into Mexico. With Stewart Hunt's influence and resources in Mexico, Jack believed that he would have been safe there. He had obviously decided that he wanted nothing further to do with New Mexico's criminal justice system. Fortunately for all concerned, Jack did not, on this occasion, find the assailants.

After their marriage in 1918, Jack and Sally left the Guadalupe Canyon Ranch and settled for several years on a small ranch north of Douglas. While there, their first child, a daughter named Dorothy, was born in 1920. Jack and Sally then moved to Bisbee where Jack reluctantly took a job in the copper mines. Their second child, a daughter named Nellie, was born in Bisbee in 1922. At about this time the Hunt Brothers' business relationship with Stewart Hunt ended, and in the process the Hunt Brothers acquired from Stewart the Malpais Ranch in the San Bernardino and San Simon Valleys. The Malpais is located off US Highway 80 about 25 miles northeast of Douglas. The Hunt brothers also acquired an adjoining ranch called the Weber Place. The stock brand for the combined properties was the I V Bar. Jack and Sally moved to the Malpais Ranch, where they were living when their third child, Thomas, was born in 1924. Elizabeth (Bess), the last of their four children was born in 1926.

Jack and Sally continued to live on the Malpais Ranch until 1937 at which time they joined Joe and family on the Honeymoon Ranch. The Honeymoon was a good and profitable ranch, but it sprawled over 110 square miles of remote, mountainous terrain. After Joe's death, Jack found it difficult to manage the ranch alone. The Honeymoon Ranch was sold in 1941, and Jack returned to Cochise County. He purchased the Double A Ranch near Tombstone and lived there until his retirement in 1950. Jack then moved to Tucson where he died in 1957.

## JAMES WILKINS HUNT

Jim Hunt was the oldest of the four Hunt brothers directly involved in the cattle ranching business. Being the most senior, he was also recognized as the leader. Jim was born in 1878 in or near McKinney, Texas, and grew up on the family farm near Comfort, Texas. He arrived in Southeastern Arizona about 1898. Initially, he worked as a copper miner in Bisbee. However, he soon began operating a livery stable in Bisbee, and not long thereafter, got into the cattle ranching business with his younger brothers and their cousin, Stewart.

He was not present at the scene of the Bartell shooting, but he was vitally involved in the aftermath. However, his name does not appear in the newspaper articles and other records of the trials. The explanation for his absence from the trial records may be found in an account related by his daughter, Susan Elizabeth (Betty) Kaye. According to Betty, Jim Hunt was called to testify at some court proceeding in connection with the Bartell matter. It was probably the preliminary hearing, for which we have found essentially no record. Jim was a very bright, competent cattleman, but he had a volatile temperament. Under hostile questioning by the prosecutor, Jim reportedly became so agitated, that he threw a chair at his tormentor. After this incident, it seems likely that the attorneys determined that Jim would not make a good witness in subsequent hearings. This could explain why Jim's name does not appear on the witness lists or in the other records and reports for the two district court trials.

After the "troubles" began, Jim continued to live in Douglas and is believed to have also spent a good part to his time over the next few years ranching in Mexico with his cousin, Stewart. In 1921 he married Mary Frances (Mae) McKinney. Their only child, Betty, was born in 1922. At about this time Jim and family took up residence on the Weber Place, the small ranch which was combined with the Malpais to form the I V Bar Ranch. When Jack and Joe departed for the Honeymoon, Jim remained on the I V Bar, where he achieved some distinction as a breeder of purebred Hereford bulls. The I V Bar was sold around 1943, and Jim and Mae retired to a home in Douglas. Jim died in the early 1960s.

It seems appropriate at this point to recount another Jim Hunt story. My late brother, Joe (also called Phil), had a strong interest in the Hunt family history, and he made notes about some of the things he had heard and knew about the subject. The following is a verbatim excerpt from Joe's notes.

> *An old family friend, Charlie Dillman had gone into Mexico with his father when he was 6 yrs old (about 1893). He had spent most of his working life running ranches for the mining companies in Mexico. He worked for Jack D. Hunt and I when we built the corrals and crossed cattle out of Mexico at Douglas in 1955.*
>
> *Charlie told me this story in 1955 and was surprised I hadn't heard anything about it. The Hunts were driving a herd of cattle out of Mexico closely pursued by one of the Mexican armies. The cattle were bedded down to rest one nite, and as was customary a rear guard was always posted several miles on the back trail. This particular nite [the guard was] Uncle Jim. As Uncle Jim was returning to the herd at daylight he came upon two advance scouts for the pursuing Mexican Army trying to locate the herd. Charlie Dillman said, "They showed fight and Jimmie had to kill them."*

We have no way of verifying this terse little story from Charlie Dillman, but we have no reason to doubt it. To say that the Hunts were killers would be something of an overstatement. On the other hand, when their vital interests were at stake, it was best not to trifle with them. The Hunts had adapted to their time and place, a social environment in which a little fierceness was an asset.

## STEWART HUNT

Stewart Hunt was born in or near the town of Como in Panola County, Mississippi on July 10, 1872. He grew up on a farm near Comfort, Texas. His previously mentioned cousins (Charlie, Jim, Jack, Sam and Joe) lived nearby. Around 1890, Stewart struck out on his own. He kicked around West Texas and Northern Mexico for several years. He arrived in Southeastern Arizona in the late 1890s at about the same time as his cousin, Jim.

He got into the cattle business early on. He spent most of his life and had most of his success in Mexico. He is reputed to have made and lost several fortunes, but he eventually died a wealthy man. He is believed to have been married three times, but had only one child, a son named Joseph or Pepe. At one time or another, Stewart owned at least three large ranches in Mexico and was involved in a variety of other business ventures on both sides of the international border. Some of these were joint ventures with his Hunt cousins (Jim, Jack et al.) and in others he partnered with his brother and members of his mother's family. He became a Mexican citizen, spoke fluent Spanish and, unlike his Hunt cousins, was very comfortable operating in Mexico. Stewart was living on the Guadalupe Canyon Ranch when Bartell was killed. He, like Jim, was not at the scene of the Bartell shooting, but as owner of the Guadalupe Ranch, was deeply involved, and suffered financially.

*Stewart Hunt, circa 1950.*

About 1922, Stewart returned to Mexico where he went on to achieve great wealth, prestige and political influence. Stewart Hunt died in Agua Prieta, Sonora on January 6, 1958. He was a remarkably bright, energetic and enterprising man, about whom too little has been written. Stewart Hunt is pictured above.

## W. H. (HUT) TAYLOR

We don't know a whole lot about Hut Taylor and his clan. They had a ranch in the Animas Valley located a few miles north of the Hunt ranch. Around 1919, Hut Taylor left the Animas Valley and he died in about 1920. Taylor and his sons had a rough and unsavory reputation. The Hunts thought they were cattle thieves and despised them. Another group of Taylors operated a ranch in Cottonwood Creek just west across the Arizona border from the Animas Valley. We think these Taylors were related to Hut. To add to the confusion, a Dan Taylor and his family lived for a time on the Guadalupe Canyon Ranch. We don't believe that Dan was related to Hut Taylor.

## THE McDONALD FAMILY

The McDonalds were pioneer Arizona cattle ranchers. Cora Bartell was a McDonald. The McDonald family was related in several other ways to the Hunts' adversaries in the Animas Valley. Hut Taylor and Henry Eicks were in-laws. The McDonalds also had some familial connection to Chap and Lee Howard, Lee Ramsey and Tobe Lacey. With these family connections, the McDonalds undoubtedly had some antipathy toward the Hunts. However, we have found no indication that the McDonalds (other than Cora) actively participated in the conspiracy to drive the Hunts out of the Animas Valley. The McDonald clan still owns and operates a cattle ranch in the extreme southeastern corner of Arizona, and many of them are buried in the Cottonwood Creek Cemetery. The Cottonwood Creek Cemetery is located in Arizona, just off the Geronimo Trail and a few miles west of the Arizona-New Mexico Border.

## WILLIAM BENJAMIN (BEN) ROBERTSON

Our knowledge of Ben Robertson is sketchy. He reportedly came to the Animas Valley from Texas in 1894, and took up a homestead near Cloverdale around the turn of the century. He worked for the Gray Ranch for many years, and at the time of the Bartell shooting,

Robertson was the manager of the Gray ranch. During his tenure, the Gray ranch, or Diamond A, was owned by the Kern County Land Company. Robertson's employment by the Kern County Land Company ended about 1926. The parting was apparently not friendly. He eventually accumulated his own substantial ranch in and around Cloverdale. Ownership of Robertson's ranch passed into the hands of one or more of his children, and they continued to operate the ranch until about 2001. I have indicated that Ben Robertson was a scoundrel and was part of the conspiracy to drive the Hunts out of the Animas Valley. This is based primarily on family lore, but the Hunts were not Robertson's only detractors. Admittedly, there is nothing in the murder trial records that directly indicate that Bartell and the Taylors et al. were in league with Robertson. Robertson was listed as a witness in the first trial, but he did not testify.

## CHESTER E. BARTELL

Our knowledge of Bartell is also sketchy. His son's birth certificate gives his age as 28. The son was born in 1915, so Bartell was apparently about 30 when he was shot on September 13, 1917. The *Lordsburg Liberal*, however, lists his age at the time of his death as "about 35". On his son's birth certificate (It is barely legible.), Bartell's place of birth appears to be Texas. The birth certificate also states Bartell's occupation to be that of a blacksmith.

Bartell's wife, Cora, stated in her testimony at the trials that they had come to the Animas Valley from Arizona in July of 1917. Prior to that, they had lived for several years in Southeastern Arizona, most of the time on ranches belonging to Cora's relatives. Before that, we think that Bartell may have lived in or near Nogales, Arizona. The Bureau of Land Management records show several Bartells having acquired patents for homesteads near Nogales in Santa Cruz County.

*Grave marker for Chester E. Bartell in the Cottonwood Creek Cemetery.*

In addition, my cousin, Tom Hunt, once encountered an individual from Sonoita (also in Santa Cruz County), who claimed to be a relative of Chester Bartell. This individual also had knowledge of Chester Bartell's having been killed by someone named Hunt.

According to testimony at the murder trials, the homestead that Chester and Cora Bartell were living on in 1917 was located immediately north of the Blair Place. Thus, their homestead was four or five miles north and west of the Hunt home at the Eldridge Place. We are also certain as to where Bartell was buried. We found a grave marker in the Cottonwood Creek Cemetery, which reads, "Chester E. Bartell—died 1916". He actually died in 1917, so the "1916" is an apparent error. The grave marker is an engraved piece of corrosion-resistant metal and is obviously of fairly recent origin (See Photo No. 5 above).

*Gravestone for Cora A. Mobley (widow of Chester Bartell) in the Cottonwood Creek Cemetery.*

I have been told that Norman Bartell, who was the son of Chester and Cora Bartell, spent most of his life in and around Douglas, Arizona. There, he reportedly owned and operated a bar and night club called the "The Little Red Barn." Norman is now dead. He is said to have had a son, Chester, named apparently after his unfortunate grandfather. The whereabouts of this latter-day Chester are unknown.

## CORA A. BARTELL

According to her death certificate, Cora Agnes McDonald was born in Toyah, Texas on February 11, 1889. Cora's mother was a Fairchild, another longtime ranching family in Southeastern Arizona. Although born in Texas, Cora must have spent part of her youth on the family's cattle ranch in the extreme southeastern corner of Arizona.

Some time after the death of her first husband (Chester Bartell) Cora married again. This time to a rancher named Lynn Mobley. She lived for the rest of her life with Mobley on a small ranch north of Douglas. Cora died at age 56 on December 29, 1945. She apparently died of injuries suffered in an automobile accident. Cora and Lynn Mobley are also both buried in the Cottonwood Creek Cemetery. (See Photo No. 6 on page 96.)

Lynn Mobley was on good terms with his Hunt neighbors, and somewhat surprisingly, Cora eventually became friendly with the Hunts as well. Tom Hunt, remembers her as a large, outgoing and somewhat raucous blond. And so we come to the final, striking irony. When Joe S. Hunt ran successfully for the office of state senator in 1934 and again in 1936, Cora Mobley was his campaign manager.

# Concluding Thoughts

Eighty-eight years have passed since the untimely demise of Chester Bartell, and all of the principals have long since died. The "troubles" were an unpleasant memory for the Hunt family, and they didn't like to talk about it. Having the detailed trial and appeal records did provide a lot of good, reliable information, but the taciturnity of our elders and gaps in the written records still leave some questions unanswered. A few of these questions are raised and discussed below.

What was going through the minds of Jack, Sam and Joe Hunt immediately after Bartell had been shot? What did they plan to do about the body? They could have loaded the body on Bartell's horse and taken it to their ranch headquarters. Did they think, if the body were left on the ground in what was a remote area, that wild critters and other natural processes would soon consume, scatter and alter Bartell's remains beyond recognition? I suggest that, in their highly charged emotional state, they were simply flustered, didn't know what to do, decided to do nothing, and left the area. Why did Sam and Joe ride on to the Gray Ranch instead of returning home with Jack? Their fear of ambush may have been real, but there was plenty of open country much closer at hand. Were they going well out into and down the Animas Valley to the Fitzpatrick, where they could be seen by others? They may have done this, hoping to create the impression that they had not been in the vicinity of the shooting scene that day.

According to their testimony in the trials, Jack, Sam and Joe were driving about 12 gentle cattle to a new watering place, when they encountered and shot Bartell. Does it really take three experienced cowmen to drive a few gentle cattle a short distance along an established trail? It seems that any one of them could have handled that task by himself. Could it have been that they were traveling together for self-protection? Or maybe it was a joint expedition to find and deal directly with those who had fired at them in recent days. If so, the encounter with Bartell may not have been entirely unexpected. As we have seen, the Hunts had a predilection for taking such matters into their own hands.

Jack must have been shocked by Cora Bartell's appearance at the Hunt Ranch house on the afternoon of September 13. If he had not thought so before, Jack obviously then realized that Bartell's death had to be promptly reported to the authorities, and proceeded to Cloverdale for that purpose. Particularly curious is the apparent failure of Jack and his sister, Bess, to mention to Cora that they already knew of Bartell's death.

The district attorney, particularly in the first murder trial, seems to have been especially vigorous in charging and prosecuting the Hunts. To what extent was he influenced by local politics? The Kern County Land Company (Kern County) owned the Gray Ranch and other large cattle ranches in the vicinity. Kern County was thus a big taxpayer and employer in the sparsely populated counties of Southwestern New Mexico. Kern County's financial clout likely translated into political clout as well. Although they were much smaller operators than Kern County, the Hunts had a good-sized cattle operation in the south end of the Animas Valley. Their cousin, Stewart Hunt, had also brought in a sizable herd to his nearby ranch in Guadalupe Canyon. Trying, not alone convicting, two of the Hunts for murder would and did seriously impair the Hunts' ability to compete with the Kern County's Gray Ranch for the grazing of cattle on the region's public lands.

What are we to make of the fact that one of the prosecutors, C. C. Royall, was reported to have been the special prosecutor for Mrs. Bartell? She no doubt wanted the Hunts to be punished for killing her husband, but why did she feel compelled to pay for legal services that should have been publicly funded? How did she pay those services? Her trial testimony indicated that she and Chester Bartell had been living a pretty hardscrabble existence. Did she receive some hidden financing from Ben Robertson and his employers at Kern County?

In his supplementary instructions to the jurors in the Silver City trial, Judge Ryan made reference to the jurors "personal interests." Intended or not, could this have caused the jurors to consider the personal consequences of acting against the interests of their powerful neighbors, i.e. the owners of the Gray Ranch? As previously noted, the New Mexico Supreme Court certainly seemed to think so. Did the political winds shift in the Hunts' favor when their case arrived on appeal in the State Capitol in Santa Fe? The Supreme Court took great pains to criticize the coerciveness they found in Judge Ryan's supplemental instructions to the jury. Do we perceive some populist sentiment here? The court may have been venting its displeasure with the disproportionate influence of the wealthy and powerful. The use of armed thugs to intimidate small landholders was a scourge in much of the American West. The unfairness of this was strongly resented by many—including, very possibly, the justices on the New Mexico Supreme Court. The ugly specter of the Lincoln County Wars and the depredations of Billy the Kid and his ilk may still have been hanging over New Mexico. An oversight by the defense apparently precluded the Supreme Court justices from using the flawed jury instructions as a basis for overturning the murder convictions. They were, however, able to justify reversal of the murder convictions by citing the improper communication between the trial judge and jury. Had they been so inclined, it seems that the Supreme Court could have found that improper exchange to have been inconsequential.

It is harder to read politics into the successful appeal of the manslaughter convictions, which came out of the second trial in Lordsburg. The issues there seemed to be more technical than philosophic. However, had they wanted to, it is conceivable that the Supreme Court could have accepted the attorney general's arguments and sustained the manslaughter convictions. They didn't.

The court decisions aside, were Sam and Joe justified in killing Chester Bartell? Well, probably not. When Sam and Joe encountered Bartell, they seemed to have had the drop on him and, if so, they didn't really need to shoot him at all. How many times did they shoot him? We have one more bit of evidence on that point. Many years later, in one of his rare comments on the "troubles," Jack Hunt told my brother, Joseph P. Hunt, "The S.O.B. had a lot of holes in him." However, ten or more bullet wounds does seem unlikely, unless you accept the defense attorneys' contention that the Taylors added a few more bullet holes to Bartell's lifeless corpse. Bartell was buried three days after he was killed, and his remains were never examined by a medical professional. In fairness to Sam and Joe, they had good reason to be fearful on September 13, 1917, so there was an element of self-defense in what they did. But whatever the precise number of wounds, it seems clear that their gunfire was excessive, and the indication of some malice on the part of Sam and Joe is almost inescapable.

One is struck by the disparity between police investigations then and now. Constable Johnson and Justice of the Peace Carriere may have been well intentioned, but both were apparently ordinary cowmen, who had little training and were, at best, only part-time public officials. Today, even the most rural of lawmen usually have extensive professional training. The murder scene, under current procedures, would have been roped off, photographed and thoroughly inspected by trained investigators. Modern authorities would not have turned Bartell's body over to his relatives, until after it had been carefully examined by a forensic pathologist. The Hunts' pistols would now be seized and subjected to ballistic testing. Such rigorous, modern-day procedures would have clarified the questions of who shot Bartell and when. And the Taylors would not, if indeed they did, have been able to fabricate additional bullet hole evidence against the defendants.

Forensics aside, it appears that the established principles and rules in criminal court procedure (presumption of innocence, inadmissibility of hearsay, right of appeal and so forth) have little changed since the murder trials of Sam and Joe Hunt. It is comforting to note this consistency in an institution critical to the governance of a free people.

In reading the records of both trials, I have the impression that both the State of New Mexico and the defendants were competently represented. Despite some bombast, the appeal briefs and other documents prepared by the attorneys for both sides were generally well written. I felt that Mr. Mathews and his defense team were particularly eloquent.

Finally, did Bartell deserve to die? Well, again the short answer is no. On the other hand, he was hardly an innocent bystander. It seems clear that Bartell did, or intended to, assault the Hunts with a firearm. And this brings to mind the old adage, "He who lives by the sword shall die by the sword."

# Timeline

**September 13, 1917**

**Chester Bartell** was shot and killed.

**March 6, 1918**

**Indictment** was issued by Grand Jury for Jack, Sam and Joe Hunt for the murder of Chester Bartell

**April 1–8, 1918**

**The murder trial** of Jack, Sam and Joe Hunt was held in the 6th Judicial District Court in Grant County (Silver City). Trial ended in **acquittal** of Jack and conviction for **second-degree murder** of both Sam and Joe.

**April 9, 1918**

**Extensive article** on trial was published in *Silver City Independent.*

**April 13, 1918**

Sam and Joe Hunt were **sentenced 40 to 50 years** in New Mexico State Penitentiary; appeal to New Mexico State Supreme Court was granted; both defendants were freed on bail set at $25,000 each.

*continued on next page*

**March 19, 1920**

Second degree murder convictions of Sam and Joe Hunt were **reversed** by State Supreme Court and **remanded for new trial**.

**May 23–26, 1921**

Sam and Joe tried again for **murder**, this time, in 6th District Court in Hildalgo County (Lordsburg). Convicted of **manslaughter**.

**May 27, 1921**

Sam and Joe were **sentenced 7 to 9 years** in the New Mexico State Penitentiary; appeal to Supreme Court was granted. Defendants were freed on bail in the amount of $5,000 each.

**January 21, 1925**

Manslaughter convictions of Sam and Joe were **reversed** by State Supreme Court, with order to discharge the defendants.

**February 21, 1925**

Pursuant to the Supreme Court order, the 6th Judicial District Court in the County of Hildalgo, **discharged** the defendants.

# Appendices

# Appendix A

**The following is essentially a verbatim transcription of a decision rendered by the New Mexico Supreme Court and published by the Court in New Mexico Reports, Volume 26. The only departures from the published report are some minor editorial changes and the omission of most of the precedent citations.**

---

SUPREME COURT OF NEW MEXICO

State v. Hunt, 26 N. M. 160.

(No.2341. March 19.1920.)

(Rehearing Denied June 8, 1920.)

STATE v. HUNT et al.

SYLLABUS BY THE COURT.

1. It is within the discretion of the trial judge to admit in rebuttal, or at the time for rebuttal, facts and circumstances which are not strictly in rebuttal, and which should be. or, might have been offered in chief.

2. An additional instruction to the jury upon their reporting to the court their inability to agree, calling the attention of the jury to the expense to the County and the defendants of the trial, the length of time it had taken to try the case, and which told them it was their duty to agree if an agreement was possible without any juror violating his conscientious conviction, was not erroneous.
3. It is improper for the trial judge to have any communication with the members of the jury about the case on trial which is not in open court and in the presence of the defendant.

Appeal from District Court, Grant County; R. R. Ryan, Judge.

Samuel L. Hunt and Joseph S. Hunt were convicted of murder in the second degree, and they appeal. Reversed, and remanded for a new trial.

EDWARD R. WRIGHT, of Santa Fe, WILSON & WALTON, of Silver City, JAMES S. CASEY, of Tyrone, and CLIFTON MATHEWS, of Bizbee (sic), Ariz., for appellants.

0. 0. ASKREN, Atty. Gen., and N. D. MEYER, Asst. Atty. Gen., for the State.

## OPINION OF THE COURT

ROBERTS, J. This is an appeal from a conviction of murder in the second degree. Three grounds of error are relied upon for a reversal. The first is in the admission of certain evidence in rebuttal. The deceased, Chester Bartell, was killed by the appellants along a trail through the forests of Grant county. The killing was admitted, and self-defense was interposed as justification. In rebuttal two witnesses were permitted to testify to the finding of a bullet at the scene of the homicide more than six months after the date thereof, and the bullet was put in evidence. The objection is urged here, and also it is further contended that the finding of the bullet more than six months after the homicide was so remote in point of time as to make evidence thereof inadmissible. This second ground is here urged for the first time, and, under the well-established rule, is not available to the appellants.

[1] As to the question whether there was error in the admission of this evidence in rebuttal when it should have been put in in chief, it is well settled that it is within the discretion of the trial .judge to admit in rebuttal, or at the time for rebuttal, facts and circumstances which are not strictly in rebuttal and which might have been offered in chief.

[2] After the jury had deliberated for approximately 18 hours without arriving at a verdict, and had then been called into Court and interrogated by the judge, and in response to his inquiries had informed him that they stood then as they had stood since their first ballot, the judge gave to the jury the following instruction:

> "Gentlemen of the jury, upon your report that you are unable to agree in the cause which has been submitted to you, I feel it my duty to direct you to consider the case further in an effort to reach an agreement. I instruct you that this case has occasioned a great deal of trouble and involved great cost alike to Grant county and the defendants. It has taken up over a week of the time of this court. It is important, therefore, both to the state and to the defendants, that you arrive at some verdict. You should agree upon a verdict. No juror, from mere pride of opinion hastily formed or expressed, should refuse to agree, nor should any juror surrender any conscientious conviction founded on the evidence and the instructions allowed and given by the court. It is the duty of each juror to reason with his fellows concerning facts in the case and application of them to the instructions of the court with an honest and fearless desire to arrive at the truth and with a view to reaching a verdict. It should be the object of all of the members of the jury to arrive at a verdict and to that end to deliberate together with calmness, reason, and fairness. It is your duty to agree upon a

verdict, if such an agreement be possible, without any juror violating his conscientious conviction. I instruct you that you should so agree without any juror violating his conscientious convictions, but let such juror reason honestly with himself whether his opinion expressed in the jury room is a conscientious conviction, based upon the facts in the case and the law as given by the court, fairly, honestly, and fearlessly considered; and you should understand very clearly that such a conviction is not determined in any wise by regard for any personal consideration involved, whether of friendship or business; and no juror should consider what may be the probable result upon any personal interest of his of the verdict that might be agreed upon. If he is guided by such personal interest, he is not faithful to the oath he has solemnly taken in this court. To aid you in further consideration of the case, I instruct you that, although the verdict to which a juror agrees must of course be his own verdict, the result of his own convictions not a mere acquiescence in the conclusion of his fellows, yet, in order to bring 12 minds to a unanimous result, you must examine the questions submitted to you with candor and with a proper regard and deference to the opinions of each other. You should consider that the case must at some time be decided, that you are selected in the same manner and from the same source from which any. future jury must be, and there is no reason to suppose that the case will ever be submitted to 12 men more intelligent, more impartial, or more competent to decide it, or that more and clearer evidence will be produced on the one side or on the other. And, with this in view, it is your duty to decide the case if you can conscientiously do so. In conferring together, you ought to pay a proper respect to each other's opinions, and listen, with a disposition to be convinced, to each other's arguments, and, on the other hand, if the larger number of your panel are for conviction, a dissenting juror should consider whether a doubt in his own mind is a reasonable one, which makes no impression on the minds of so many men, equally honest, equally. intelligent with himself, and who have heard the same evidence, with the same attention, and with an equal desire to

> arrive at the truth, and under the sanction of the same oath, And, on the other hand, if a majority are for the defendants, the minority ought seriously to ask themselves whether they may not reasonably and ought not to doubt the correctness of a judgement. which is not concurred in by most of those with whom they are associated, and distrust the weight and sufficiency of that evidence which fails to carry conviction to the minds of their fellow jurors."

Before submitting this instruction to the jury, a copy of it was handed to counsel for appellants, and they stated the following objection to the giving of the instruction:

> Defendants at this time object to the giving of the additional instruction to the jury for the reason that such instruction does not state the law, in that it directs the jury to consider matters other than the evidence adduced upon the trial of this cause in arriving at their verdict, in that it is calculated and intended to give the impression that each juror should regard the opinion of the greater number of jurors as entitled to more weight and consideration than the opinion of the smaller number of jurors; that those who are in the minority should renounce their convictions and give way to the opinion of those who are in the majority, merely because of such preponderance of numbers, in that it seeks a verdict which is not in truth and in fact the individual verdict of each and every juror, in that under the existing circumstances it amounts a coercion of the jury, in that its highly prejudicial to these defendants.

If the language in the instruction by which the trial court denounced as unfaithful to his oath any juror who in forming or adhering to an opinion was influenced by personal considerations of friendship or business was calculated to coerce or intimidate the jurors, of course, the instruction would be erroneous. But it will be observed that this ground of objection was not urged in the court below, and, according to the authorities, this is the only possible error in the instruction. In the case of Territory v. Donahue, 16 N. M.17,

113 Pac.601, an instruction given under similar circumstances, and which went almost as far as this instruction, was approved by the territorial Supreme Court. The instruction here went further in this; it called the attention of the jury to the expense to the county and the defendants of the trial, length of time it had taken to try the case, and told them repeatedly that it was their duty to agree if an agreement was possible, without any juror violating his conscientious conviction, and further as above pointed out. The general rule is that the trial court may detail to the jury the ills attendant on a disagreement, the expense, the length of time it has taken to try the case, and that the ease would have to be decided by some jury on the same pleaings and in all probability on the same testimony. Case notes will be found fully discussing the question and citing all the cases as follows: Alabama Great Southern Railroad Co. v. Daffron, ....

It is very doubtful whether the court was warranted under the law in the use of language which called attention to a possible personal interest of some of the jurors in the case, or a fear of the result upon their personal interests. This may have acted as a form of coercion upon the minority of the jurors. They may have reasoned that the court was of the opinion that their refusal to agree to a verdict was prompted by personal interest or that the fear that an agreement on their part to a verdict might affect their business interests. It was unfortunate language, to say the least. But, as stated, this ground of objection was not urged to the instruction of the court below and is not available to the appellants here.

[3] It is lastly urged that it was error for the judge to have a conversation with a member of the jury about the case during a recess of the court and in the absence and without the knowledge of appellants or their counsel. but in the presence and with the knowledge of the district attorney, and in that conversation to advise the juror to rise in the jury box in open court, after all evidence and

argument. had been concluded, and request that the right shoe of the deceased be cut open and exhibited to the jury. and for the judge afterwards to grant such request when actually made in open court, never having disclosed to appellants or their counsel that such conversation had been had or such advice given.

The facts upon which this alleged error is predicated are as follows: Upon the trial of the case a shoe taken from the right foot of the deceased was put in evidence. A bullet had penetrated the sole of this shoe near the toe. It was the theory of the state that the bullet had been fired by one of the appellants while the deceased was lying on the ground and at the time of the fatal encounter. It was the contention of the appellants that the bullet had been fired into the sole of the shoe some hours after the death of deceased by one of his friends for the purpose of manufacturing evidence against the appellants. Evidence had gone in by experts the effect that a bullet fired into a dead body would not cause a flow of blood. The shoe was not cut open, and it was impossible for anyone to see whether there was or was not blood in the toe of the shoe.

The facts attending the conversation between the court and the juror were certified by the trial court as follows:

> "After the argument to the jury of Clifton Mathews, who made the closing argument for the defendants, the court announced a recess; thereupon; as the jury were leaving the jury box and before the court had retired from the bench, Juror M. N. Ross approached the judge of the court in the courtroom and stated that the jury desired to have the shoe in question opened so that the Interior thereof might be discovered and so that it might be disclosed whether or not the toe of the said shoe contained blood; that at the time said request was made the jury were in the act of leaving the jury box, the judge of the court had not left the bench. and there were several bystanders within hearing distance of the said juror, Ross, at the time he made said request, and the judge of the court

thereupon stated to said juror that, if the jury desired that this be done, the proper course to follow was for one of the jury to rise before the court in the jury box in open court and make such request; that at the time said request was so made by said juror, M. N. Ross, and at the lime the judge of the court made his statement to the said juror, M. N. Ross, in response to said request, the defendants were not, nor was either of them, and counsel for defendants were not, nor was either of them, within hearing so far as the court is aware of said juror, M. N. Ross, or of the said court, or of the said colloquy which occurred between the said juror, M. N. Ross, and the court. Counsel for the state thereupon, or immediately thereafter, knew and became aware that such request had been so made, and that such response had been so made by the court, as above recited, but, so far as the court is aware, neither the defendants, nor either of them, nor their counsel, nor either of said counsel, heard said request, or the response of the court thereto, or knew of the same. Thereafter, and after all argument of counsel to the jury had ended and closed, and before the court had instructed the jury, said juror, M. N. Ross, in open court, from the jury box, requested the court to allow said shoe, State's Exhibit D, to be so cut open. Thereupon the state, through its district attorney, assented to the same being done, and thereafter the defendants, through their counsel, assented to the same, and thereupon, after such assent in open court, the said shoe was by the sheriff, under the direction of the court, cut open, so that its interior, which was not previously disclosed to view, could be seen, and when said shoe was so cut open, and the interior thereof so exposed to view, there was visible in that part of said interior so exposed to view, at and around and near the bullet hole passing through the sole of said shoe, a considerable quantity of dry blood, or of a substance having the appearance of dry blood. Said shoe, State's Exhibit D, was thereupon passed into the jury box, and in such condition was viewed and examined by the members of the jury, and thereupon, and immediately thereafter, the court proceeded to instruct the jury and to give them the case for consideration of their verdict."

It is elementary that in a felony case the accused must be personally present at every stage of the trial. If any material step in the trial is taken in his absence and a conviction results, it must be set aside. This rule has been applied in many cases. It has been held, for example, that it was fatal error to proceed with the impaneling of a jury in the absence of the accused. Warfield v. State ....

It is likewise reversible error to permit any evidence to be heard in the absence of the accused. State v. Moran....

So also must a conviction be set aside where the accused was absent during the argument to the jury. Tiller v. State....

Absence of the accused while the judge is instructing the jury is equally fatal. Roberts v. State....

In like manner a verdict of guilty rendered in the absence of the accused must be set aside. Harris v. State....

As a part of the same doctrine, it is uniformly held to be reversible error for the judge to have any communication with the jury, except in open court and in the presence of the accused and his counsel. A case in point is that of Territory v. Lopez, 3 N. M. 156, 2 Pac. 364. The defendants in that case were being tried for cattle stealing. After the jury had been charged by the court, and had retired to deliberate, they were brought into court, in the absence of the accused and their counsel, and one or more of the number made an inquiry of the judge as to where those men," meaning the defendants, "were driving those cattle," and the judge, in the absence of the accused and their counsel, answered the inquiry by telling the jury that they must determine that fact according to the evidence and just as they would determine any fact in the [sic] own private affairs. There was a verdict of guilty, and on appeal the Supreme Court said:

> "The defendants were being tried for grand larceny, which, under our law, is a felony. The doctrine seems to be well settled, that after the jury have been instructed and have retired to consider

of their verdict, in all trials for felony it would be irregular and improper for the court to receive the jury, or to have any communication with them touching the case submitted to them, in the absence of the defendant. In all such cases the presumption of law is that the irregularity per se constitutes error. On this subject Mr. Bishop says: 'It is a principle pervading the entire law of procedure in criminal causes that, after indictment found, nothing shall be done in the cause in the absence of the prisoner.' 1 Bish. Crim. Proc. § 682. To this principle, as a rule of law, there are no exceptions other than in the lower class of misdemeanors, where a fine only, and no corporal punishment, may be imposed, and in a few instances of orders within the discretion of the presiding judge, such as an order on a motion for a continuance. And even such motion, if made on behalf of the prosecution, cannot be entertained, except on notice to the prisoner or his counsel. Id. §§ 684, 685. In regard to felonies Mr. Bishop further says: 'In felonies it is not in the province of the prisoner, either by himself or by his counsel, to waive the right to be personally present during the trial.' Id. § 686. This is strong language, but It is unquestionably the law. * * * After the jury have been charged by the court, and they have retired to deliberate, it Is always proper for them to ask the bailiff in charge to conduct them before the court for further instructions. But in all such cases the proper practice would be to send for the prisoner and his counsel, and as soon as they come into court to have the names of the jurors called, and, if all are found to be present, the court will then receive any communication they have to make, and instruct them accordingly. Mr. Bishop more elaborately puts it thus: 'After the jury have retired to deliberate on their verdict, there may be further communication between them and the court at the desire of either. If at the court's, an officer is sent for them, and It takes place in open court; the judge has no right to visit them for the purpose in their room, or otherwise communicate with them In private. If at the jury's, they are conducted for the purpose into open court. The counsel and the parties should be notified, arid their presence is a right or necessity the same as during the prior parts of the trial. The

> Instructions desired on the one side or the other and required by the circumstances will th (sic) be given.' 1 Bish. Crim. Proc. (3d Ed.) § 1000."

It is to be conceded that therc was no impropriety in the juror asking that the shoe be cut open, or on the part of court in granting the request. The error consisted in the communication between the judge and the juror about the proper way for the jury to obtain the right to inspect the inside of the shoe in the absence of the defendant and while the court was not in session.

In an early Massachusetts case (Sargent v. Roherts, 1 Pick. 337, 11 Am. Dec. 185) the foreman of the jury sent a note to the court stating that it was impossible for the jury to agree. The judge in reply addressed a written communication to the jury urging them to agree. The note from the foreman of the jury and the written communication by the judge were filed in the case so that what was said did not depend upon the memory of the judge or juror. The court said:

> "The object of the note of the foreman was probably to obtain leave for the jury to separate, and the answer of the judge was calculated to enable them to revise the case in a systematic manner, in the hope that such a revision would produce a union of opinion on one side or the other of the cause. It probably had that effect. As it is impossible, we think, to complain of the substance of the communication, the only question is whether any communication at all is proper; and, if it was not, the party against whom the verdict was is entitled to a new trial. And we are all of opinion, after considering the question maturely, that no communication whatever ought to take place between the judge and the jury, after the cause has been committed to them by the charge of the judge, unless in open court, and where practicable, in presence of the counsel in the cause. * * * It is not sufficient to say that this power is in hands highly responsible for the proper exercise of it; the only sure way to prevent all jealousies and suspicions is to consider the

judge as having no control whatever over the case, except in open court in presence of the parties and their counsel."

Many cases to the same effect will be found cited in notes to the cases of State v. Murphy .... These cases are practically unanimous upon the proposition that any communication between the judge and the jury respecting the case, had after the cause has been submitted and not in open court and in the presence of the parties is reversible error. And this upon the ground that any communication under such circumstances is improper, and that the party in order to secure a setting aside of the verdict was not required to show prejudice, but only the fact that there was such unauthorized communication. There is no more reason for saying that it is improper for the trial judge to communicate with the jury after it had retired to consider of its verdict not in open court and in the presence of the parties than for him to have such communication with the jury about the case while on trial and prior to such retirement. Whatever fact the juror desires to communicate to the trial court relative to the case then on trial should be made from the jury box in open court and in the presence of the parties and likewise the answer of the judge thereto. For this reason the cause must be reversed, and remanded to the district court for a new trial; and it is so ordered.

PARKER, C. J., and RAYNOLDS, J., concur.

---

# Appendix B

**The following is a transcription of an article published in the *Silver City Independent* on April 9, 1918:**

## Sam and Joe Hunt Found Guilty of Second Degree Murder for Killing of Chester Bartell, a Homesteader

---

## JURY DELIBERATES THIRTY-SEVEN HOURS

---

Makes Special Recommendation to Court That Clemency be Extended.

---

## JACK HUNT IS FREED

---

State Moves for Instructed Verdict of Acquittal for Third Defendant in Midst of Trial and Puts Him on Stand; Large Number of Witnesses Give Testimony; Trial Extends Over a Week.

---

After a trial lasting six days, Samuel L. Hunt and Joseph S. Hunt, brothers, and well known young cattlemen of southwestern Grant County, were found guilty by a jury in the district court yesterday morning, of murder in the second degree, for the killing near Cloverdale, September 13, 1917, of Chester Bartell, a homesteader. The jury recommended the convicted men to the clemency of the court. Sentence will be pronounced at the close of the court term.

The verdict came after the jury had deliberated for 37 hours. It looked like the jury would be unable to agree for, after having been out 18 hours, it was called into court Sunday evening at 5 o'clock by District Judge Raymond R. Ryan and reported then that it had stood 9 to 3 since the first ballot and appeared to be deadlocked. Judge Ryan gave the jury additional instructions as provided by statute, urging that each member weigh carefully the evidence and reach a verdict if at all possible.

Again the jury retired and remained out all night Sunday and until almost noon yesterday, when it finally reached a verdict and the same was returned into court. When the verdict was read, neither of the defendants nor members of the Hunt family present, gave any outward expression of their feelings. The verdict was delivered into court by John M. Wiley, foreman.

Counsel for the defendants gave notice of a motion for a new trial. If this is denied the case will be appealed to the state supreme court, and application for the release of the convicted men on bond will be made. In the meantime, the two Hunt brothers will be confined in the county jail. Since the killing of Bartell, Sam and Joe Hunt, as well as their brother, Jack Hunt, who was acquitted the fourth day of the trial on motion of the state and by direction of the court, had been at liberty on bonds of $25,000 each.

### Great Interest in Trial.

The trial of the Hunt brothers, Samuel L. and Joseph S., for murder, another brother, John P. Hunt having been indicted jointly with them for the killing of Chester Bartell, but acquitted on an instructed verdict, the fourth day of the trial on motion of the district attorney, rivaled in interest, length and the formidableness of counsel engaged, the sensational trial of the Parks brothers, which preceded it.

From the day the case was called, until it closed, the court room was filled daily with spectators and especially at the night sessions were the crowds attending unusually large. Because of the prominence of the defendants the trial attracted more than local attention.

In attendance on the trial of the defendants, were the father of the accused men, their two sisters and two brothers, one of them, Dr. W. [sic] P. Hunt being a prominent practitioner of Douglas, Ariz., and a member of the staff of the Copper Queen hospital there. Mrs. Cora Bartell, widow of the slain man, with her little son, and other relatives, also attended the trial.

Although the trial began Monday, a week ago, a jury was not secured until the following day. The regular panel of 12 men quickly was exhausted and a special venire of 50 names was drawn Monday afternoon. This, too, was exhausted and another special venire of 50 names was drawn, from which the jury was finally completed, as follows: A. C. Bibbs, Santa Rita; C. B. Munro, Silver City; H. J. Morton, Silver City; James S. Landrum, Tyrone; S. J. Hausman, Hurley; James W. Worrell, Santa Rita; Marvin Powe, White Signal; Arthur A. Burdette, Silver City; Joseph Landrum, Central; George Palmer, Hurley; M. N. Ross, Santa Rita; John M. Wiley, Silver City.

## Widow Chief Witness.

With the opening of court last Wednesday morning, the introduction of evidence began. The state placed its principal witness, Mrs. Cora Bartell, widow of the slain man, on the stand as the first witness. Mrs. Bartell related that she was married to Bartell in 1913 in Arizona, where they lived for a time. In August, 1917, they removed with their baby to New Mexico, settling on a homestead, 10 miles northwest of Cloverdale in southwestern Grant county near the Arizona line. They first used a tent for a home, later building a small frame house or shack. Mrs. Bartell said that her husband began to dig a well soon after they took up their residence on the homestead that they might have water, but found no water.

Mrs. Bartell then told of how her husband started out for the Hunt ranch, a few miles away, the morning of September 13, the day he met his death. The witness said her husband told her he would go over to the Hunt ranch, about four miles distant, and see if he could not make arrangements with the Hunt brothers for the use of a watering place on their land, for some cattle he was to bring over from Arizona. She said that he took along with him a puppy to give to the Hunt boys. The relations between Bartell and the Hunts had always been friendly, according to the testimony of Mrs. Bartell. Bartell left home, his wife testified, about 9 o'clock. She said she told him not be gone long, as their baby boy, about a year old, was sick and they had planned to take the child to Douglas to consult a doctor.

About 10:30 o'clock, Mrs. Bartell said the puppy came back to the ranch and along about 11 or 11:30 o'clock, when the baby became quick [sic] sick, she started out to find her husband, so they could go at once to a doctor, with the little boy. She said she saddled a horse and taking the baby with her, started for the Hunt ranch. According to Mrs. Bartell, it had rained the night before and she easily followed the tracks of husband's horse over the trail. She testified that when she reached the top of the ridge of mountains rising out of the valley, she observed Bartell's horse, riderless, grazing off to one side of the trail. She went over to where the horse stood and said she found her husband's Winchester in the scabbard on the saddle. She took the rifle and scabbard off the saddle and placed it on her own saddle and leading Bartell's horse, returned to the trail. She then rode carefully over the trail looking for her husband, all the while carrying her baby in her arms. Suddenly, Mrs. Bartell said, the child lisped "Daddy, mama, daddy." Looking ahead, Mrs. Bartell observed her husband's prostrate form lying beside the trail. Quickly dismounting, she went to where her husband lay on the ground, lifted his head and tried to give him some water from a water bottle she carried. However, when she touched him, she found him cold in death. Her first thought, she said, was that he fallen from his horse and been dragged to death.

Mounting her horse, she rode direct to the Hunt ranch. The first one she met, she testified, was John Hunt, and to him she reported that her husband was lying on the trail up on the mountain dead, stating she thought he had been dragged to death by his horse. The witness said that when she asked that someone go and get the body, that John Hunt replied that he would go and get an officer, and he left the ranch soon thereafter in a car. Mrs. Bartell remained at the Hunt homestead over night.

## Ignorant of Shooting.

Mrs. Bartell said she was ignorant of the fact that her husband had been shot until the following morning, when Marion and Lee Taylor came to the ranch after her and she started home. She said no one at the ranch had told her that Bartell had been shot and killed.

The night previous, evidence later introduced revealed, the body of Bartell, following an inquest held by a coroner's jury at the spot where Bartell's body was found, was placed in a wagon and taken to the ranch of W. H. Taylor. At the time of the inquest, only two bullet wounds had been found in the body, one in the left breast, which had caused death, and another wound in the right hip.

W. H. (Hut) Taylor, the next witness for the state, identified the clothes taken from Bartell's body, these consisting of a blue jumper and two pairs of overalls and shoes. He testified that Justice of the Peace Louis Carriere of Cloverdale, had brought the body over to his house and had reported finding but two bullet wounds. Carriere then left.

The body of the dead man had been placed on a cot in the yard and Taylor said his attention was attracted to the corpse the next morning by blood oozing out of the cot covers from the shoulders. This aroused his suspicions he said, and he sent his boys out to call in some of the neighbors, that they might be present when the body was undressed and a fuller examination made. About 8:00 a.m. the morning of September 14th, the day following the death of Bartell, this examination of the body was made by Taylor and his sons, with a number of neighbors as witnesses.

The witness then testified that the following wounds were discovered: A bullet hole in the left breast near the heart; two wounds in the right arm near the elbow; one wound in the left shoulder and another in the right shoulder; a wound in the left thigh; three wounds in the right hip; two wounds in the right knee and a bullet wound in the right foot. Taylor further testified that on September 15, he and Tobe Lacey went to the place where Bartell had been shot and he said they found six empty shells from an automatic revolver near the spot where the body was picked up. In Bartell's Winchester, he said, but two cartridges, unfired, were found.

Tobe Lacey next testified and corroborated the testimony of Taylor, relating he had been summoned to the Taylor home the morning of the 14th to witness the undressing of Bartell's body and its examination for bullet wounds. He said, wounds as described by Taylor had been found. He also said that he and Taylor had found six empty shells near the scene of the shooting when they visited the spot September 15.

E. W. Taylor, known by the nickname "Rat," testified about the bringing of Bartell's body to his father's home and described the numerous wounds found on the corpse, as did also James Moorehead, one of the neighbors summoned to be present at the examination, together with William Birchfield and Joe Yarborough.

## Justice Carriere Testifies.

The state next placed Justice of the Peace Carriere on the witness stand. Judge Carriere testified that on the afternoon of September 13, Jack Hunt came to his home and told him that Chester Bartell had been killed by Sam and Joe Hunt. The judge then started out with Jack Hunt to summon a coroner's jury and proceed to the scene of the tragedy to hold an inquest. On their way to the Gray Ranch, Judge Carriere said, they met Sam and Joe Hunt riding horseback along the road, about 8 miles from the scene of the shooting, both being armed. The judge said he told both boys to consider themselves under arrest and that after placing them on their honor to report when summoned for hearing, he permitted them to go home.

It was at this stage of the trial, Thursday morning, that an unexpected incident occurred. After conferring with associate counsel assisting in the prosecution, Attorneys K. K. Scott and Charles C. Royall, District Attorney Vaught, made a motion, asking the court to instruct the jury to return a verdict of acquittal as to Jack

Hunt, indicted jointly with his brothers, Sam and Joe, for the murder of Bartell, because there was insufficient evidence to warrant his prosecution. The court acted accordingly and Jack Hunt was at once acquitted and discharged.

**Jack Hunt State Witness.**

Jack immediately was placed on the stand by the state, and related the story of the killing of Bartell by Sam and Joe Hunt. Jack Hunt said that he and his two brothers on the morning of September 13, started out for a watering place about two miles from their homestead, driving a small bunch of cattle. When they reached the top of the trail, leading over the mountain, the witness said they came to a small clump of trees and bushes, around which the trail forked. Just at this point he said, several of the cows strayed to one side and left the trail. He pulled out after them on his horse, riding several hundred yards and getting out of sight of his brothers. The witness was startled, he said, by several shots in rapid succession—he could not state how many—and drawing his own six-shooter, he galloped back to the trail, believing his brothers had been ambushed. When he arrived at the spot where they were on their horses, he said both had their six-shooters in their hands and nearby Chester Bartell lay on the ground, apparently dead. His brothers told him, he said, that as they reached the top of the trail and unexpectedly met up with Bartell, that the latter had reached for his Winchester in its scabbard on the side of his saddle and that each brother, believing the other was about to be killed by Bartell, opened fire simultaneously on their would-be assailant with fatal result. The witness testified he advised his brothers they had better get away from the scene at once as there might be others lurking around there to shoot them and that Sam and Joe then started for the Gray Ranch, he going back to his own home, the Hunt Ranch, to get a car and go notify the officers of what had occurred. He told of Mrs. Bartell later coming to the Hunt Ranch and reporting she had found her husband's body, and asking him to get someone to go and bring it in. Witness said he told her he would go get an officer. He was examined at considerable length by counsel for the state in an effort to bring out all the facts connected with the shooting of Bartell. With the conclusion of Jack Hunt's testimony, the state rested.

## Defense Offers Evidence.

The defense started the presentation of its evidence by placing Justice of the Peace Carriere, of Cloverdale, on the stand. Judge Carriere testified relative to Jack Hunt notifying him the afternoon of September 13th, of the shooting of Bartell by Sam and Joe Hunt and of later going to the scene and holding an inquest. He said that he made a careful examination of the body of the dead man and found only two bullet wounds. He said he also found an empty shell from a 45-calibre automatic pistol about three feet from the body and a water bottle. He said the left shoe was off the dead man's foot. He went into other details regarding the removal of the body to the Taylor home. On cross-examination, the District Attorney Vaught subjected the witness to a vigorous questioning. The district attorney asked the witnesses if it was not a fact that in February, this year, he had not stated to him in the presence of Jesse Cook, C. C. Royall and Herbert J. McGrath that he did not make a careful examination of Bartell's body; that the examination took place at night on the mountain trail and that he and the coroner's jury had only a smokey [sic] lantern and a flashlight to aid them. The witness denied any such statement.

Jack Sims, the next witness, gave testimony along the same line as that of Judge Carriere, saying the coroner's jury had made a careful examination at the time of the inquest and found only two wounds on Bartell's body. On cross-examination, Sims would not swear that there were only two wounds on the body. He also denied that he had testified before the grand jury that the examination of Bartell's body was made in the darkness with a smokey lantern and a flashlight. Bert Rhodes, another of the coroner's jury, testified that he saw only two bullet wounds on Bartell's body and swore positively to this. On cross-examination, he admitted having been with the Hunt brothers considerably since the killing and was friendly with them. George Parish and Munro Dunagan, two more of the coroner's jury, testified they had found only two bullet holes in Bartell's body.

Miss Elizabeth Hunt, a sister of the defendants, testified that she was at home at the ranch the day Chester Bartell was shot and killed and related how Mrs. Bartell had come to their ranch. She said Mrs. Bartell had told her about finding her husband's body on the trail on the mountain and that Mrs. Bartell further stated that when she went over to where her husband's horse was standing, she found his Winchester partly out of the scabbard on the saddle.

## Tells of Arresting Hunts

Charles Johnson, constable of the Cloverdale precinct, next related how he proceeded to the Hunt homestead about midnight on the 13th day of September and placed the Hunt brothers, Sam, Joe and Jack, under arrest. He testified he was there early the next morning when Mrs. Bartell left with the Taylors and that she carried a six-shooter, wrapped in a webb belt, which she handed to Lee Taylor. Jack Sims also testified having seen a six-shooter strapped around the waist of Mrs. Bartell.

Dr. O. J. Westlake gave expert testimony regarding the effect of rigor mortis on a human body and gave it as his opinion that the body could not be easily handled after death had ensued, say from eighteen to twenty hours. He also said that a dead body would not bleed. Here the state sprung a surprise, when K. K. Scott, cross-examining Dr. Westlake, handed him the clothes taken from the body of the dead man and had him identify blood stains on the clothes, asking him if the stains were made before or after death. Dr. Westlake testified that in his opinion they were made before death, excepting possibly a blood stain on that part of the overalls which covered Bartell's left thigh.

## Three Brothers Testify.

Jack Hunt then took the stand and related, without material change the story he had previously told of the shooting when called to testify by the state. Next, Sam Hunt went on the stand and told practically the same story of the shooting of Bartell as had been told by his brother, Jack. Then, Joe Hunt testified and his story of the actual shooting corroborated the story already told of the killing by his two brothers. However, Joe further testified that Bartell had been shooting at him on previous occasions and because of these attacks all three brothers had gone armed to defend themselves. The witness swore he shot Bartell in self-defense, believing that Bartell meant to kill either his brother, Sam or him. He said that both quit shooting as soon as Bartell fell from his horse. None of the stories told by the three brothers were materially shaken on cross-examination by counsel for the state.

The defense closed its case by putting a number of character witnesses on the stand to prove the previous good character and high standing of the two defendants in the community in which they lived and also in the state of Arizona, their former home. These character witnesses included J. E. Brophy, of Bisbee, Ariz.; John E. Evans, of Tyrone; William Riggs of Douglas; William Birchfield, of Animas; Charles Johnson, of Cloverdale; Holmes Maddox, of Animas; and M. E. Cassidy, of Bisbee.

### Evidence in Rebuttal.

On rebuttal, the state presented material evidence. S. Ernest Pollock, undertaker and embalmer, testifying as an expert as to the effect of rigor mortis on a dead body, stated that it did not affect broken bones. Jesse Cook and District Attorney Vaught then testified as to statements made to them by Judge Carriere in February, this testimony being offered to impeach that given by Judge Carriere on the stand. Miss Frances Nutt, grand jury stenographer, then testified as to statements made before the grand jury by Jack Sims, her testimony being offered to impeach testimony by Sims.

Mrs. Cora Bartell was recalled by the state and testified that on September 7, 8, 9 and 10 her husband was with her on their homestead, that he was digging a well and was not away from the place, her testimony being offered to disprove Joe Hunt's testimony that Bartell had been shooting at him on these days while he was riding over the range. Mrs. Bartell also testified that at the suggestion of the district attorney she had again visited on March 15 the scene where her husband was shot and killed, in company with her uncle, Davis McDonald, and Bert Black and that at the spot where her husband's body was found they had dug in the ground and found a steel-jacketed bullet about an inch in the ground, the point of which was flattened by contact with a rock. The bullet was introduced as an exhibit.

Next, Marion Taylor was called and testified that on the 15th of September he went to Bartell homestead at the request of Mrs. Bartell to get some mules and said that he found Bartell's six-shooter, in a scabbard and belt, wrapped around the head of the bedstead. This evidence was tending to prove that Bartell had no six-shooter with him the day he was shot, and also to prove that Mrs. Bartell was not seen wearing it. Jake New corroborated Taylor's testimony regarding the finding of the six-shooter. Davis McDonald testified about being with Mrs. Bartell and finding the bullet buried in the ground at the spot where Bartell was killed. It was at this stage the state closed its case, Friday night, and court recessed until Saturday morning, to permit counsel to address the jury.

### The Closing Arguments.

When court convened Saturday morning at 9:00 o'clock, Attorney Charles C. Royall, special prosecutor for Mrs. Bartell, made the opening address on behalf of the state, speaking for 40 minutes. Mr. Royall summed up the evidence of both state and defense and presented the case to the jury for final decision. Mr. Royall was followed by James S. Casey, of Tyrone, of counsel for the defendants. Mr. Casey consumed 45 minutes in his arguments to the jury and briefly but clearly reviewed the evidence presented. His address was an excellent one on behalf of his clients. Attorney K. K. Scott, who assisted the district attorney, next addressed the jury and he talked for an hour and twenty-eight minutes. Seldom had a stronger argument been made in a Grant county court room than that made by Mr. Scott and his summing up of the case was a telling one from the state's standpoint. Attorney Percy Wilson of the Wilson of the Wilson & Walton firm, next spoke to the jury on behalf of the defendants and ably presented the case of the defense, going into the evidence in detail and summing up all the testimony offered. He spoke a little more than an hour. Following Mr. Wilson, Clifton Matthews, of the law firm of Ellinwood & Ross, of Bisbee, Ariz., chief counsel for the defendants, addressed the jury. It was the first time Mr. Matthews had been heard in a Grant county court room. His remarks to the jury embraced a complete rehearsal of all the evidence presented at the trial and an earnest plea for the acquittal of the defendants. His effort was a masterly one. He spoke for four hours and twenty minutes. For the state, District Attorney J. H. Vaught closed the arguments and in the half hour that he talked to the jury he went into the essential details of the case and summed up the evidences clearly. The arguments took up the entire day and extended well into the night.

Judge Raymond R. Ryan thereupon read his charge to the jury. This had been carefully prepared being unusually lengthy, and required almost an hour for delivery. When Judge Ryan had finished, one of the jurors, M.N. Ross, requested that the bullet-pierced shoe introduced as an exhibit, be cut open for inspection by the jury and this was done, counsel for both sides interposing no objection. When the shoe was slit open, it had a large clot of blood in the toe and the lining was blood-stained. The jury retired shortly before 11:00 PM to begin its deliberations.

# Appendix C

**The following is a transcription of an article published in *The Lordsburg* (New Mexico) *Liberal* on May 26, 1921. The article was copied verbatim, ignoring any errors in spelling, punctuation or syntax.**

---

## "MANSLAUGHTER" IS VERDICT OF JURY

**First Petit Jury in Hidalgo County Declares Hunt Bros. Guilty of Manslaughter. Judge Mechem Sentences Each to the Penitentiary 7 to 9 Years. Appeal Is Made to Supreme Court and Bonds Fixed at $5,000.**

The Second trial of the Hunt Brothers, Samuel L. and Joseph S., commenced in the district court of Hidalgo County, Monday morning, Judge Edwin Mechem, of the third district, a brother of Governor Merritt C. Mechem, presiding.

District Attorney Forest Fiedler and former District Attorney J. S. Vaught representing the state and Attorneys Wilson and Walton of Silver City and Attorney Clifton Mathews, of Globe, Arizona, the defendants.

The entire first day and evening was spent in selecting a jury, with the result that was very satisfactory to both sides. This took a special venire of eleven men, chosen just before the afternoon adjournment. The jury finally selected included:

D. C. Banta, Rodeo,
A. J. Love, Rodeo,
E. M. Fisher, Lordsburg,
G. F. Dean, Rodeo,
Harry A. Cook, Rodeo,
H. H. Bartlett, Lordsburg,
S. F. Allen, Lordsburg,
Dave Sprouse, Valedon,
I. A. Bradberry, Lordsburg,
C. Russell, Valedon,
Albert Hill, Lordsburg.

The second day was consumed by the State, the first witness being Mrs. Cora Bartell, widow of the deceased, the other witnesses being Amos Taylor, Fred Sanford, Joe Yarbro, W. P. Birchfield, Jr., J. H. Moorehead, W. M. McDonald and Jack Hunt. Each witness was cross-examined by Mr. Mathews for the defense.

The defense put on as regular witnesses Jack Hunt, Sam and Joe Hunt, defendants; Mount Manning, Wm. Swyer, and Don S. Sullivan.

As character witnesses the defense called Capt. Harry C. Wheeler, Chas. E. Cross, Capt. M. E. Cassidy, Prof. Harry Crockett, M. E. Cassidy [sic], Wm. P. Birchfield, Jr., and Holmes Maddox. The character witnesses were put on at the session last night, following which the State put on some rebuttal testimony leaving the arguments of counsel until this [sic].

The Liberal never cares to go into grewsome [sic] details of an alleged murder. The simple facts as brought by the testimony are enough.

According to the State's witnesses the late Chester Bartell was shot and killed on the morning of Sept. 3, 1917, by Sam and Joe Hunt, all three men being on horse back on the Coronado Forest in the southern part of Grant (now Hildalgo) County. There was no eye witnesses except the ones who are alleged to have done the shooting, and according to the testimony all of the men were armed with Winchesters, the defendants having revolvers as well.

The defendants admit firing the fatal shots, Sam firing five shots from his six-shooter and Joe firing more or less from his.

There was no effort made to escape. On the other hand, the defendants gave themselves up to officers of the law, alleging that their act was done in self defense, as the deceased was in the act of taking his Winchester from its scabbard attached to his saddle, when they fired. Joe testified that it was his belief that the deceased had fired at him on two or three occasions a few days prior to the unfortunate tragedy.

The case was tried before Judge Ryan at Silver City, in April 1918, at which time the jury brought in a verdict of second degree murder, the Supreme Court subsequently granting a new trial, and as the county of Hidalgo is now separated from Grant, the second trial was held here.

The first address to the jury by counsel was made for the State by District Attorney Forrest Fielder, who presented in a plain, straightforward manner what the State should expect at the hands of the jury. It was Mr. Fielder's first appearance here in a big case and he made a most favorable impression.

Mr. Fielder was followed by defendant's attorney, Clinton Mathews, whose powerful and eloquent plea for his clients, who as friends, were more than clients, brought tears to many eyes. It was pronounced by everyone a masterpiece, doing honor to the man who gave it utterance.

Attorney W. B. Walton followed for the defense with a fair and impassioned plea. The former congressman fully sustained his reputation as a lawyer of large calibre.

The closing plea for the State was made by Attorney J. S. Vaught, and is counted by bench, bar and people as one extraordinary merit. Many grasped his hand at the close and said, "I never heard anything better."

Judge Mechem gave some very carefully prepared instructions to the jury and sent them to the jury room to consider the evidence.

After being out all night the jury agreed upon a verdict of Manslaughter. According to members of the jury the first ballot stood, 4 for second degree murder, 4 for manslaughter and 4 for acquittal. The last ballot before the final ballot, it is stated, stood 11 for manslaughter to 1 for acquittal.

Judge Mechem passed sentence at 9:30 Friday morning, giving each defendant 7 to 9 years. An appeal was immediately taken to the Supreme Court and the bond was fixed at $5,000 each.

The case was very ably and very fairly conducted on both sides and the presiding Judge bore out his reputation as being impartial and just on the bench.

---

## IMPORTANT COURT NOTES

---

### S. R.O. Sign In Court

Standing room only has been in order most of the trial.

### McDonalds Here With Niece

David and W. M. McDonald, uncles of Mrs. Bartell, are with her during the trial.

## Judge Winter Here Tuesday

Judge W. H. Winter, of Las Vegas was here Tuesday to confer with Judge Mechem.

## Hunts Don't Use Tobacco

Dr. C. H. Hunt, J. W. Hunt, J. P. Hunt, S. L. Hunt, and J. S. Hunt, brothers, are non-tobacco users.

## Lawyers All Friendly

"I never saw lawyers so friendly in the trial of a big case," said a court attendant. "I haven't seen them quarrel once."

## Blondon and Foley, Bailifs

Wm. Blonden and Harry Foley are serving as bailifs, it being their duty to have entire charge of the jury night and day.

## Jack Hunt Double Witness

John C. Hunt, a brother of the defendants, is a witness for the State and for the defense. He's a mighty fair witness, at that.

## Ladies Attend Trial

A good many ladies are attending the trial. Likewise, quite a number of high school students, who have taken great interest in court procedure.

## "Tom" Helping "Bob"

Former County Clerk Tom Holland is assisting County Clerk Reynolds during the court session. Tom was clerk during the former trial of the Hunts in Grant County.

## Perpetual Mayor Wilson

Percy Wilson, one of the attorneys for the defense, has been mayor of Silver City every since he was a "kid." He is serving now his 17th consecu- [line missing in original] mighty well or else he's got 'em hipnotized [sic]. Looks like they like him.

## Prof. Crockett Teaches Printing

Prof. Harry Crockett, character witness, is instructor of

printing in the Bisbee Schools, where they have a linotype and regular printing plant. Prof. Crockett is a linotype school graduate and practical printer.

### Burns Case Dismissed

The case of alleged blackmail against B. F. Burns, of Animas, was dismissed by the court, upon motion of District Attorney Fielder. Mr. Burns expects to leave in a few days for California to spend a few weeks with relatives.

### No Reflected Light Necessary

Judge Edwin Mechem don't have to have to shine by any reflected light of his distinguished brother, Governor Merritt C. Mechem. He's one of those 100-per centers on his own hook. Upon his return home Saturday, he will be greeted by the governor and their mother in sort of a family reunion.

### Arizona Legal Light Here

Clifton Mathews, of Globe, of the law firm of Rice & Mathews, is trial attorney for the defense. He is considered one of the sure-enough legal lights of our neighboring state. His conduct of this trial would fully sustain this reputation. He's a sure "good 'un."

### Attending Officers

The officers in attendance are Sheriff Oscar Allen, Chief Deputy Earle Kerr, Clerk R. M. Reynolds and stenographers Mrs. Ada Estes Woodbury and Mrs. Elmer E. Thede. Mrs. Woodbury, who is the regular stenographer, was taken ill the second day and Mrs. Thede came from Deming to help out the court.

### A Pathetic Figure in Court

Without reference to the merits of the case, a pathetic figure in court is Mrs. Chester Bartell, widow of the man who lost his life and her little son,

Norman, who was with her on the horse when the body was found. The little chap was only 24 months old when his "daddy" was killed.

### "Billy" Walton on the Job

Former Congressman, former Senator and for years unnumbered, political "factotum" of New Mexico, is one of the defense lawyers. Everybody gives Walton credit or [sic] being one of the hardest working members of Congress the state ever had. He's also past Grand Master New Mexico F. & A. M. and knows every nook and corner in the state.

### Camp Cody Morale Officer Here

With the Bisbee friends of the Hunts, is one of the prominent officers of Camp Cody, Capt. M.E. Cassidy, Camp Morale officer under Gen. Lindsey. The Liberal editor was publicity director for the camp and had much aid from Capt. Cassidy. In civil life he has charge of all accident settlements for the P-D Corporation at Bisbee. He uses the same brand of good sense for P-D, that he did for the U.S.

### Vaught is Trial Lawyer

District Attorney Forrest Fielder has as his assistant, in the capacity of trial lawyer, former District Attorney, J. S. Vaught, who conducted the state's case in Grant County, when the defendants were convicted in Judge Ryan's court, and a new trial granted by the Supreme Court. According to the court records, Vaught has been very successful in the trial of criminal cases. He is just fresh from the trial at Silver City, when the youthful prisoners were convicted of murder in first degree, Jailer Bencomo being the victim.

### Hunts Have Many Friends

Just to show how well the Hunt boys are thought of at home, a delegation of character witnesses volunteered to come over from Arizona, including Capt. Harry Wheeler, Capt. M. E. Cassidy, Prof. Harry Crockett of Bisbee Schools and his wife, Mr. and Mrs. John B. Rawlings, formerly of Bisbee, now with the C. & A. Co., at Valedon, former Deputy Sheriff Chas. Cross, of Bisbee; Mrs. E. B. Rider and Miss Bessie Hunt, sisters of the defendants and their guest, Miss Alice Crone, of New York; W. A. Nowlin, a brother-in-law; Miss Kennedy and Earl B. Thompson, of Bisbee. The Hadalgo County character witnesses are W. P. Birchfield, Jr. and Holmes Maddox, the well known ranch men of the Upper Valley.

## Look, Who's Here

Capt. Harry Wheeler, the Sheriff with a backbone who said to the Bisbee I.W.W's ; "You git" and they got while the getting was good.

"Capt. Wheeler is a mighty likable chap, although like adamant against lawbreakers. He was an overseas officer and had a brother in the Rainbow Division who came home with 30 wounds on his body, and yet a pretty good man physically. Gene Mantague introduced the captain to E. A. McElgin, whose brother received fatal wounds in the same company of the Rainbow Division. They had a mighty good visit. Small world this.

Capt. Wheeler has fallen in love with Lordsburg hospitality and says his trip over here on behalf of his friends, the Hunt brothers, is worth $500 to him. "I like to meet your kind of people," he said to the *Liberal*. They're worth while."

# Bibliography

## Books

1. Gray, John Plesent, author, and W. Lane Rogers, editor, *When All Roads Led to Tombstone: A Memoir,* Boise, Idaho, Tamarack Books, Inc., 1998.
2. Hilliard, George, *One Hundred Years of Horse Tracks: Story of the Gray Ranch*, Silver City, NM, High-Lonesome Books, 1996.
3. Dunagan, Lenora and Carol Dunagan Smith, *To Animas With Love,* Dexter Michigan, Thomson-Shore, Inc., 2004.
4. Hayes, Alden, *A Portal to Paradise*, Tucson, AZ, The University of Arizona Press, 1999.
5. Supreme Court of New Mexico, *New Mexico Reports No. 26, Appeal No. 2341, State v. Hunt, et. al.*, published by the Supreme Court of New Mexico, Santa Fe, NM, pp. 160–170, March 19, 1920.
6. Supreme Court of New Mexico, *New Mexico Reports No. 30, Appeal No. 2901, State v Hunt, et. al.*, published by the Supreme Court of New Mexico, Santa Fe, NM, pp. 273–276. December 22, 1924.

## Newspapers

1. "N. M. Court Orders Two Released Held for Manslaughter," *Bisbee Evening Ore*, December 23, 1924.
2. "Killing in Southern Grant County," *The Lordsburg Liberal*, September 21, 1917.
3. "Killing on State Line," *Silver City Independent*, September 18, 1917.
4. "Court Session to Last Eight Weeks," *Silver City Independent*, March 12, 1918.
5. "Hunt Murder Case Called for Trial," *Silver City Independent*, April 2, 1918.
6. "Sam and Joe Hunt Found Guilty for Second Degree Murder for Killing of Chester Bartell, a Homesteader," *Silver City Independent*, April 9, 1918.
7. "Hunt Brothers Found Guilty of Murder in Second Degree," *The Lordsburg Liberal*, April 12, 1918.
8. "Sam and Joe Hunt Found Guilty by Jury," *The Silver City Enterprise*, April 12, 1918.
9. "Men Convicted of Murder Sentenced," *Silver City Independent*, April 16, 1918.
10. "Criminal Docket Over in District Court," *The Silver City Enterprise*, April 19, 1918.
11. "Untitled Article", *Silver City Independent*, April 23, 1918.
12. "Untitled Article," *Bisbee Daily Review*, April 11, 1918, page 8.
13. "Date Set for Trial of Hunt Brothers," *The Lordsburg Liberal*, May 19, 1921.
14. "'Manslaughter' Is Verdict of Jury," *The Lordsburg Liberal*, May 26, 1921.

# Supreme Court Records

1. Case No. 2341, State of New Mexico, Appellee, v. Samuel S. Hunt, et al.,
   Appellants:
   Transcript of Record
   Brief of Appellants (printed)
   Brief of Appellee
   Reply Brief of Appellants (typewritten)
   Reply Brief of Appellants (printed)
   District Court Extension Orders (3)
   Appearance of Appellant
   Motion for Extension, February 17
   Stipulation
   Motion for Extension, April 19
   Motion for Rehearing and Brief
   Appellant's Reply Brief on Motion for Rehearing
   Opinion of the Court
   Receipt for Mandate
   Copy of Mandate
2. Case No. 2901, State of New Mexico, Appellee vs. Samuel L. Hunt, et al, Appellants:
   Transcript of Record
   Brief of Appellant
   Brief of Appellee
   Reply Brief of Appellant
   D.S. Extension Orders (8)
   Appearance for Appellants
   Motion
   Notice
   Acknowledgment of Service

Stipulation
Stipulation
Request for Oral Argument
Acknowledgment of Service
Copy of Mandate
Receipt for Mandate
Opinion of the Court

## Certificates

1. Bartell, Male Child, Arizona State Board of Health, *Certificate for Birth*, January 3, 1915, Douglas, AZ.
2. Mobley, Cora Agnes [Bartell], Arizona State Department of Health, *Standard Certificate of Death*, December 29, 1945.

## Joe's Notes

Listed below is the index to a transcription of handwritten notes prepared by my brother, Joseph Phillip Hunt. The notes relate to various aspects of our family's history. Most of the notes were based on Joe's memory of various anecdotes, which he had heard from his parents, uncles and other family members. Apparently, the notes were still a work-in-progress at the time of Joe's death in 1999.

1. Hunts Come to America
2. Grandad Hunt
3. Grandad's Brothers
4. Grandmother Hunt
5. Life in Texas
6. Oklahoma
7. Arizona / Sonora—Early Days

8. Uncle Charlie
9. Search for the Toyopa Mine
10. New Mexico
11. Ranching Along the Border
12. Steward Hunt
13. The Mormons
14. Eagle Creek
15. The Kennedys

# Interviews


1. Finley, Dorothy Hunt—Hunt Family History, Various Dates
2. Hadley, Diana—History of Guadalupe Canyon and surrounding area, May 25, 2004. June 14, 2004, February 23, 2005 and September 30, 2005.
3. Hadley, Drummond—Cattle Ranching in and around Guadalupe Canyon, November 20,21, 2004.
4. Hunt, Thomas—Hunt Family History, Various Dates
5. Kaye, Susan (Betty) Hunt—Hunt Family History, Various Dates
6. McDonald, William W.—Cattle Ranching in Southeastern Arizona and Southwestern New Mexico, October 29, 2005.